Whispers of the Demon

By

Nakhon Hanchawa

Copyright © 2024
All Rights Reserved
ISBN:
Hardcover: 978-1-962381-52-9
Paperback: 978-1-962381-51-2

Dedication

I would like this book to be dedicated to Perry Craig Rohan, the love of my life; Theodoor Bolten, who helped me proofread; friends and family; and all the angels who keep protecting and guiding me.

Acknowledgment

From my experience, not exactly but close to what I expected. I'm extremely satisfied. Thank you again!

About the Author

I have shared my personal journey and shed light on the diverse lifestyles of transgender individuals, offering a glimpse into different perspectives.

Contents

Dedication i

Acknowledgment ii

About the Author iii

Chapter One 1

Chapter Two 17

Chapter Three 51

Chapter Four 91

Chapter Five 111

Chapter Six 127

Chapter Seven 145

Chapter Eight 161

Chapter Nine 179

Chapter Ten 197

The page left blank Intentionally

Chapter One

Adrian never knew how warm blood could feel until that very moment when it dripped from her forehead. One of the kids had managed to pelt a stone straight to her head, and blood was dripping fast. At first, she felt the impact and fell to the ground. Feeling the warm sensation on herself is what made her cry immediately. It didn't stop the children. They continued pelting stones. Adrian got up and ran, sobbing the entire way home.

More stones hit her back, her arm, but finally, after what felt like ages, they stopped. Adrian felt her lungs on fire and her legs tire. But she couldn't stop. If she did, they'd come back again. Heaving like mad, she saw her house in the distance and forced herself to pick up her pace. For an eight-year-old, the girl had garnered tremendous speed. She'd lie to her parents about winning races at school, which is what made her fast when the truth was the other kids didn't let her near them and would prefer chasing her down.

Rushing through the back door, she entered the kitchen and dashed for the dark store room. It was pitch black, which she preferred. Sobbing in a corner, she pressed her back to the wall and slid down, letting the tears roll. Adrian had to be careful, though, so as not to draw her parents' attention. Mum and Dad had been arguing the entire night and had fired up again in the morning. Adrian never fully understood what the fight was about, but her siblings insisted on not getting in the way. On an occasion or two, her brothers tried to and got smacked pretty hard. Adrian followed.

Adrian started fighting back her sobs and stepped out of the store room, reaching for a glass and pouring herself a glass of water. This required her to climb a chair, fetch a glass from a cupboard, climb down, and pour from the mug. Even at that young age, she had to learn how to go about doing this herself since her brothers and sisters would get irritated with helping her. If something went wrong, she'd have to face her parents' wrath.

Gulping down the glass, she poured another. Adrian went to the sink, washed the glass, and looked around to see if there was any company. The house was oddly quiet. Since it was evening, that only meant one thing.

Her siblings were out playing with their friends, Dad had still not returned from work, and Mom was probably out walking or buying groceries. The silence made the house feel cold and unwelcoming. Adrian looked around at her family photos and those of her grandparents and relatives. Some of them were in black and white, which bluntly hinted at how far away time they were taken. Yet, it wasn't the lack of color that bothered her; it was the fact that no one smiled in their photos. There was one with her when she was a baby, in her mother's arms, surrounded by her siblings. Her father wasn't present, since he had to take a photo. Adrian's sister, Lu, would tell her that Dad didn't want to be in the photo, which is why he deliberately chose to take a picture rather than be next to his family. Her brother Lee told her it was because Dad was upset about having a girl.

This is where Adrian would get confused about the versions of the story. Lee mentioned that Dad was upset because he had wanted a son, but Lu mentioned that she was first a boy and then a girl. It made no sense. Was she born one thing and then changed somewhere in between? When Adrian tried bringing this matter up with her grandparents, they did what they usually did give her the silent treatment. The little girl always felt like she had done something wrong, but no one would tell her what that was. The elders in her family didn't want to acknowledge her presence, and it came to the point that her mother ordered her to stay in her room until the elders left.

The girl felt the tears welling up again as the faces of the bullies came up again. She wouldn't get attention from her family, and the peers who gave her attention would only be in the form of mean words and inflicting pain. Adrian would go crying to her eldest brother, Chai, but he always seemed embarrassed by her. Every kid on the block was scared of Chai since he was the fastest and strongest boy around. If anyone tried to mess with him, his friends, and even his siblings, they'd have to face his fists. That notion came to a halt when it came to Adrian. On one occasion, he, in fact, pushed her into the mud when she asked for his help regarding a boy who wouldn't stop pulling her hair.

"Stay away from me, freak!" Chai screamed. "I don't care what Mom and Dad say; you're not my sister!"

Seeing little room for her own company, Adrian spent time on her own. It was a rare thing when her siblings wanted her company. They seemed content with one another and their friends. There wasn't much insistence from her parents when it came to having everyone play together.

Adrian fought back her sobs and felt her forehead. The blood was still oozing, and now the cut area felt worse. She made her way to the bathroom sink. Climbing on a plastic chair, she looked to see the damage. A major chunk of the blood had dried all over her hair, much of it giving her hair a red flair. The cut wound was now surrounded by a blueish color that ached every time she tried to touch it. The girl washed her face carefully and reached for the gauze. Pulling a piece, she dabbed some Dettol, only to spill most of it in the sink. Mom was going to kill her now, for sure. She looked at the wound in the reflection and started dabbing.

The sizzling burn made it all the more difficult, and she started crying again.

"I want Mommy," she whimpered, trying to heal her

wound.

Whether she slid the Dettol-infested piece of cotton or dabbed it slightly, the burning sensation remained the same. The silence became prevalent again, and Adrian could hear her whimpers echoing in the house. No one was home. No one will be. No one would care if she was hurt. Her saddened face turned angry, and she pressed the gauze hard into her wound, letting the burning escalate. She kept it there for almost a minute till she couldn't take it anymore.

Sobbing some more, Adrian placed a band-aid on her wound, hoping it would be enough. With her business done, she went to her room and lay down on her bed. Whatever tears she was restraining now finally came pouring with ease. The girl kept crying and wishing that the mean kids got a taste of their own medicine.

"One day," she sobbed, "I will be so big and strong that everyone is going to be scared of me."

The running, crying, and fantasizing tired the little girl, and soon enough, she was asleep. Dreams were always a shaky matter for Adrian. Sometimes, she would have the best one ever, but most of the time, nightmares would consume her. Monsters and ghouls would be chasing her down, and she would be crying for her mother. Her mother, at best, would only cradle her till she went back to sleep.

Adrian found herself luckily in a nice place. It was her

birthday, and everyone was singing around her. Mom made her favorite chocolate fudge cake while her dad helped her cut the cake. Her siblings clapped their hands and sang song after song as if stuck on a loop. Adrian was relieved that her dreams were being kind to her. Unfortunately, this moment of happiness was short-lived.

Adrian woke up to the sound of yelling from downstairs. She rushed down the stairs to find her parents having a shouting match. Dad had already thrown one of the chairs against the walls in frustration, breaking its legs. Chai emerged from the corner, rushing to stand in front of his mother. Lou and Lee joined, but it didn't help calm the situation. If anything, the sight of the kids aggravated the patriarch even more.

"Stay away!" Chai threatened, trying to look intimidating.

"I am your father!" he roared. "Show me some respect!"

"Please don't hurt Mama!" Lu cried.

Adrian watched with dread, clinging to them tightly with nervousness. At any minute, this entire day could take a very ugly turn, and she didn't know what to do. Her father had already started roaring and breaking more things to scare off the kids, but something inside her compelled Adrian to run and stand right between the line of fire.

"What the hell are *you* doing?" her father seethed. "Get back to your room where you belong!"

"No!" Adrian gulped. "I... I won't let you hurt Mommy or my brothers and sisters."

"Like the way you fended off those kids?" her father spat, pointing to her band-aid. "Can't hold your own, and now you're gonna challenge me?"

Adrian couldn't move. Whether it was bravery or fear, she remained solid. She looked back at her mother, who was already confused about what she was doing. The girl thought for a quick moment and stepped forward, surprising everyone in the room.

Adrian reached for her band-aid and, in a quick swipe, revealed her wound, which had now turned quite ugly. The sight of it took her father aback. He looked at his daughter as if she were looking at her for the very first time. Shock and awe.

"The kids did this to me!" Adrian spoke. "Despite that, I am here standing against you. They can't break me. Neither can you. So, if you want to hurt my family, you have to go through me."

Her father stared. His eyes shifted from Adrian to his wife and kids. They were still whimpering, and his wife was shaking from head to toe. Something about Adrian's words seemed to have resonated something in him. His tightened fists loosened, and he simply walked out the door. Adrian watched, confused.

Right before he reached the door, Adrian feared the worst. If he went out, he might never return. One moment, she was fighting him off, and now she charged to hug his legs. The girls wailed and cried.

"Please don't go!" she sobbed. "Just say sorry to Mommy, and all will be okay again."

No such thing happened. Her father picked her up, and she cried in his arms. Her mother was now calming Chai, Lu, and Lee. Adrian watched as her father laid her on the bed. An automatic reaction kicked in, leading the girl to feel ridiculously sleepy than before. The moment her head lay on the pillow, she noticed her father wanted to say something but stopped midway. He stared outside the window as if pondering over something important.

Adrian was about to say something to break the silence, but he noticed her immediately.

"Who were the kids who did this to you?" he asked.

Adrian remained silent.

"I'm not going to ask twice."

Seeing little choice, Adrian complied.

"The ones who live three houses down." She spoke.

"Stay away from them. Understand?"

Adrian nodded, scared.

With that said, he got up.

"Get some sleep."

The man walked outside, and the sound of scurrying went around. She noticed Chai walk, and without any warning, he smacked her in the head, making the girl cry.

"Don't ever do something stupid again!" he said. "We're all lucky it didn't get worse."

"I helped stop the fight."

"No! You just delayed it. Now, what they didn't say to each other today will be said tomorrow. Thanks a lot, dummy."

He left, hitting her hard in the tummy and left. Adrian lay there crying herself to sleep. She wanted to help, but now her big brother let her have it. The girl prayed that tomorrow would just be the slightest bit different. She hummed a tune to herself that let the dreams return.

Adrian had a house she could return to, but she had a hard time calling it a 'home.' Most of the kids around her would talk about what their parents got for them for their birthdays or the places they would go to during vacations. For her, that was never the case. Birthdays were barely celebrated, and gift-giving was a rare thing. Adrian had still not received any toys, whereas the others had.

"You're not special," Lu would spit at her.

Adrian would run to her mom crying but would only get a few reassuring pats and was told to either play or finish her homework. This became a pattern, so the little girl came to realize that when it came to her feelings, it was better to keep it to herself. Her parents were too busy, and her siblings didn't really care.

Since the weekend had come, Adrian didn't have to go to school, much to her relief. She had never liked it since day one, and the kids kept getting meaner. It was an odd sight when her teacher also seemed to be at a loss on what to do with her. At best, she was made to sit in a corner and read, write, or draw. Adrian noticed she was good at it than the other kids and picked up on things faster than the others. That garnered appreciation from the teacher but spite from the other kids.

"Stop showing off!" Chang would say, hitting her.

Soon enough, Adrian decided to remain silent unless spoken to. At one point, she deliberately started giving the wrong answers just to avoid Chang confronting her. It didn't help. He, along with his friends, would pick on her during recess, and it was cleverly done in hidden corners so they wouldn't get into trouble.

Adrian made it a point to spend time on her own, walking by herself and spending time outdoors. Saturday had come around, and the outside world was inviting her. She was supposed to do her chores, but her memory slipped because the outdoors looked too tempting to ignore. Clouds covered a major chunk of the sky, and the sunlight beamed through slightly.

Adrian loved staring at the sky and wondered what it would be like to jump and bounce on those soft-looking clouds. Maybe someday, when she was older, she would learn to fly those planes she would see now and then. They would take her wherever she wanted to go.

Adrian passed by the marketplace and found herself close to the river. It was always nice and serene there. The water was always crystal clear, and green grass covered both sides of it. Adrian loved catching the fish, twirling around her feet in the cold water. Some of them would start dancing around her ankles, while the others kept pecking at her toes. Most of the time, she didn't feel anything, but every now and then, she'd start giggling once the ticklish tingle started passing in.

This time, the fish were oddly more keen than usual, and Adrian found herself laughing as she walked across the water. A few big ones would come around, and she would grab them quickly. Some were lucky to swim away, but others had to endure being held in her hand, wriggling around like crazy before she would put them back in the water.

"Go be free!" she chimed with a smile.

Adrian was having the time of her life playing around until her eyes fell on a stranger standing close by. He was poorly dressed and looked filthy. Even from a distance, Adrian could smell his stench. He was a repulsive sight, and that bothered the girl.

"You!" he snapped, pointing at her, while the other hand reached his pocket. He pulled out candy from his large pocket from a torn coat. "I give candy. Come here."

Adrian was warned excessively by her parents about talking to strangers. Comparatively more than her siblings. The girl wasn't sure as to why they insisted that she needed to take extra care of herself because other people wouldn't 'understand.' She didn't understand it when they explained it to her but nodded either way. Now, with the stranger standing in front of her, she felt very comfortable. The girl looked around and could tell there weren't other people present.

"Come on now," the stranger insisted, "It's yum-yum."

The old man put one into his mouth without removing the wrapper and started chewing. After some chewing, he smiled. Adrian had never seen such rotten teeth before, and she was already moving away.

"Hey!" the stranger said, getting aggravated. 'Listen to your elders!"

The change of tone was all that Adrian needed to know that she had to run. This stranger did not have good intentions, and she felt it in her gut. She ran as fast as she could, while the old man began to follow. His run was as awkward as it was slow. The man could barely lift his legs. It seemed he was just shuffling his feet fast. This gave the girl ample opportunity to get ahead, and soon, she was screaming and crying for help.

Luckily for her, she managed to reach the marketplace in time. The man was still hot on his heels, but when Adrian ran to the first shopkeeper, he immediately took action.

"Stay behind the counter!" he instructed.

Adrian followed his instructions as the man went out and fired his gun in the air before taking aim at him. Adrian watched from behind the glass of the counter as the stranger cursed first but immediately changed course when the gun was aimed at him. At first, he continued shouting slurs at the shopkeeper when he turned away, but the moment the gun went off and the shells missed him by a little distance, he fled. His stunted legs seemed to have found the stability he needed, and in moments, he was gone.

Once the shopkeeper returned, Adrian ran to him, held

him tight, and bawled. Unlike her parents, this man had more of a soft spot.

"It's alright, child," he reassured her. "He's gone now. Let's get you home."

The kindness of others was something Adrian was not quite used to, but this man had earned her trust instantly. He held her hand and walked her home while some peering eyes followed them. Some people even whispered to one another, while others asked what just happened. Since it was a small town, word would spread fast. People were already making assumptions. Adrian felt everyone's judgmental eyes on her as they walked, but the shopkeeper's presence made her feel safe. A part of her longed that this walk would last forever. Unfortunately, not all wishes come true. The shopkeeper knocked on her door, and Adrian's mother opened it.

"Dao?" she said, confused. "What are you doing here? Adrian? Go to your room this instant!"

Adrian was two steps in before she turned and hugged Dao tight. He smiled and patted her head.

"Now!" her mother growled.

Adrian followed orders. Her mother and Dao started talking, and the last thing the girl noticed was the uncomfortable expression on Dao's face as he explained.

Adrian spent the rest of the day in her room waiting for

dinner. She would kill time drawing until her mother stormed in furious.

"What the hell were you thinking?" she shouted.

Within moments, Adrian was covering herself from the frequent smacks coming at her.

"Have I not taught you anything! Didn't I tell you not to speak with strangers!"

"I didn't, Ma!" Adrian pleaded. "I didn't know who he was."

"Now you're lying to me! You had chores to do, and you instead went out without my permission?"

The intensity escalated, and Adrian begged her mother to stop. Unlike the usual spanking, there was something spiteful about this one. Her mother kept yelling and hitting her until she was tired. With her breath heaving, she grabbed her daughter's wrist and pulled her to meet the eye.

"What happened today will bring shame to this family!" she seethed. "Because of you, everyone in this house has suffered. Get one thing clear in that skull. You are an *unnatural mistake*! Remember that."

Her mother smacked her with force and pushed her to the bed.

"An unnatural mistake." She repeated before closing

the door.

It had only been a few hours, and Adrian was made to believe that she was a curse on her family. She knew that there was something oddly different about her at that moment. This act of hers would stay with her for the rest of her life. Little did she know that a lot awaited her in the time to come.

Chapter Two

Adrian smiled ear to ear once her teacher placed her test paper on her table. A big fat 'A' with a personal note from her was written. When it came to academics, the girl never had a hard time. Her peers and her siblings would tend to cringe at her success, yet at the same time, many asked her for help when needed. Adrian never turned them away because it made her feel important. It was something she was good at, and everyone knew it.

Plenty of people assumed that Adrian studied hard because she wanted to make an impression, but the truth was quite different. She knew that the only way to get away from her family and home was through the means of education. She had heard stories about some seniors who performed so well that they pursued a life in a country called America.

Adrian was quick to find out all that she had to about this country across the ocean that had so much to offer. It was a place where dreams come true. People across the globe would flock to it because it always had something to offer. Having skimmed through books in libraries, Adrian learned that the country certainly had its fair share of baggage. A long history of violence and discrimination was there, but at the same time, there were movements to protect those being harmed. The suffrage movement and civil rights proved to her that there was hope for improvement. Many communities over the years had been moving there; maybe now she had her chance.

Now fifteen years old, Adrian began to experience many changes like most kids did. The boys around her got taller and grew thin mustaches, while the girls grew breasts. Their behavior even began to change. Some who were quiet became chatterboxes, while troublemakers became quiet. Some remained the same, while others changed partially. The one person Adrian noticed that really experienced a change was Deng, a shy one, who grew and was now getting plenty of attention from the girls. This gave him a bit of confidence, but he still maintained his distant nature.

Adrian looked at others and then herself. Something wasn't quite making sense when it came to her body. It was hard for her to explain in words, but it seemed that she had both the anatomy of girls and boys. While her face appeared feminine and petite, her body displayed more toughness than it should. This led to plenty of ridicule in her direction. When she was a kid, bullying was a common feat. Now, it had become the bane of her existence because everyone felt the need to remind her how *unnatural* she was.

"Lady boy!" she would hear sometimes.

Adrian dreaded wanting to know what that word meant. The kind of spite it carried hurt her more than any of the other mean words that came her way. The girl had now grown accustomed to her own company and spent most of her time either buried in books or walking about. The mean kids had changed their approach to her. They preferred staying away rather than causing physical harm. Yet, Adrian dreaded that something ugly was coming her way. Having experienced nothing but hurt from others, she felt it was only a matter of time.

The house she resided in was quieter than ever. Her father experienced a stroke some years back, which placed him on bed rest. Doctors assumed he would be up and running in a few weeks, but it seemed that the attack had wounded more of the man's spirit than his body. His rested on the pillow, and he barely moved a muscle. Adrian's mother may have carried some pity, but that was replaced with apathy.

"At least the house won't be as noisy." She spat.

Her siblings kept themselves busy in their own lives. With the patriarch now unable to afford the house, Adrian's brother took it upon themselves to work. Soon, the sisters joined in. Adrian would prefer helping out in the house, but with the atmosphere becoming sullen, she went over to the shopkeeper to give her something to do.

On most occasions, he would have her delivering goods from the shop. He paid her for the effort but preferred having her doing the accounting. Her grip over the numbers impressed him, and it certainly lessened his work at the end of the day. Deng never liked the mundanity of numbers, and it required him to stay at the shop longer since his wife never wanted him bringing work home.

Adrian managed to kill time with studies and work, but that routine did come with its fair share of loneliness. She had mastered the art of getting by, but the need for companionship grew even more. It seemed that her wishes were being heard because once summers ended, a new face came around her class, Jane.

Adrian knew this girl was going to be special to her. She had her fair share of crushes on boys, mostly the seniors, since they looked so much better and groomed than her peers, but this was the first time she found herself drawn to a girl. The feeling was new and unknown, making her all the more nervous and awkward.

It was the first class at 9am when their teacher guided Jane into the class. Adrian was doodling on the back of her notebook, when the teacher caught her attention.

"Everyone, this is Jane," she instructed. "Let's all be welcoming and nice to her. Remember, first impression…"

"Last impression." the class chanted.

Adrian couldn't stop staring at the sight. Cute cheeks, straight brown hair, and kind eyes, Jane smiled at everyone.

Adrian felt that was the kind of face that was made to beam. The genuineness melted her heart.

"Well, since we're limited on space," the teacher said, looking around till her eyes fell on the girl in awe. "Why don't you sit next to Adrian over there."

Adrian felt the world freeze for a moment before it immediately picked up the pace. Jane was walking towards her one moment and then abruptly right next to her. The girl did her best to pretend she was still doodling till she felt a nudge on her arm.

"Hello, neighbor," she chimed.

"Erm... hi," Adrian replied awkwardly.

"I've heard about you."

Adrian already felt her heart sink. What was there to say about her in a place like this?

"Nothing good, I assume." Adrian sighed.

"Actually, I was told that you're the smartest one in class. Always getting the best marks."

"Oh..." Adrian said, surprised. Getting a compliment was a rare thing. She wondered for a moment if she was being tricked. "Well... I guess that's... nice?"

Jane looked at Adrian from head to toe as if trying to take an entire scan of the person who sat next to her.

"You're a strange one." She mentioned.

Adrian knew what was coming next. This always happened. What a fool she was to think that this person could be any different.

"I think we're going to get along just fine." Jane smiled.

At first, Adrian assumed she had heard it wrong. It was not until she turned to look at Jane smiling at her that she realized the girl was being honest. This was their first meeting, and already, the new kid in town had taken a shine to her. Adrian felt something come alive inside of her. Her tummy fluttered with butterflies that it became overwhelming. Trickles of sweat began to pour from her forehead, and her hands were slightly shaking. She had been nervous before, but there was something different about this one. Adrian was quick to react.

"Can I go to the bathroom?" Adrian said, shooting her arm up.

Some of the kids giggled as she left. Darting her way to the girl's bathroom, Adrian splashed her face with water. While scrubbing her face with soap, she noticed that the tingling was now passing through her fingers.

"What is this?" she whispered. "Am I going crazy?"

The bell rang, and a clutter of students began moving about outside. Adrian immediately dried herself with the paper and walked out. Right from the corner of her eye, she noticed Jane approaching.

"You, okay?" she asked, concerned.

There was no spite or ulterior motive in her eyes. Every word and act seemed honest. The sinking feeling in her chest brought tears to her eyes, and before she knew it, she was crying. Jane was quick to hold her.

"Hey, hey, what's wrong?" she asked.

"I'm sorry," Adrian whimpered. "It's just so much has been happening, and I can't make sense of it."

Jane noticed that most of the people passing by were looking at them strangely. It made her feel uncomfortable. Noticing the girl had a lot more crying to do, she was quick to act.

"C'mon," she insisted. "Let's get you to the nursery."

Adrian struggled to straighten herself. She didn't want to look at the expressions of the others walking past. She kept her eyes down as Jane held her gently by the wrist. It took a moment for Adrian to point out something.

"Hey Jane," she sniffled. "Nursery is that way."

"Sorry, first time here." Jane giggled.

That managed to bring a smile to Adrian's face. She wiped her tears and guided Jane in the right direction. From that day on, Adrian had found herself something she hadn't had in a very long time: a friend.

For the first time, Adrian felt a certain kind of elation that made her nervous just as much as it made her happy. Jane was not like the others. Many times, Adrian insisted that Jane find herself a different company because as long as they were seen together, they were made the butt of jokes. Unlike Adrian, Jane had the sharp wit and confidence to talk back to others.

"Oh, look at that," one of the bullies scoffed, "Adrian found herself a baby sitter."

"Hey, if you need help cleaning your pooped pants," Jane chimed back. "Adrian and I could do wonders for that diaper of yours that is sticking out."

Everyone noticed to see that boy's underwear was showing, which he was quick to hide. It was too late, everyone laughed hysterically. Adrian looked at Jane fascinated. She was met with a wink that made her blush.

The school became tolerable, and rather than spending time at the library, Adrian found herself moving about the school more often with her friend always present. It was strange that, having been to the school for plenty of time, she was looking around it as if she were the guest and Jane the guide. She didn't know there was a secret corner in the large garden where a large tree stood. Plenty of the kids would bury a box of cigarettes, which they would puff on later outside the mall. Jane and her would chuck a few for themselves without anyone looking.

They were standing alongside a truck after school hours when Jane pulled out a stick.

"You're actually going to do it?" Adrian asked, concerned. "That will kill you."

"Oh, come on," Jane replied, rolling her eyes. "You only live once. Plus, we're all going to die someday. Don't you want to put this off your checklist?"

"Checklist?"

"Like a bucket list. You jot down the things you want to do in life and start ticking one off after the other till they're all done. That's when you kick the bucket."

"Why not just keep the list? Is the bucket really necessary?"

Jane laughed at that.

"No, silly," she said. "The bucket is a metaphor."

Adrian liked the fact that she amused Jane, it's just that she always came off as naïve, maybe stupid.

"Silly me indeed." Adrian nodded.

"Hey, none of that."

"None of what?"

Jane crossed her arms and looked at her like a stern mother. She sighed, lit up the cigarette, and took a long puff meditatively. Adrian's eyes were glued to how the stick flared between her pretty, thin lips.

"You have this habit of being too hard on yourself." Jane pointed out. "It's like bullying yourself."

"Yeah, I looked it up in one of our psych books. Low self-esteem is what they call it."

"Did it tell you another thing about what you should consider before you agree to have it?"

Adrian raised an eyebrow.

"What?"

"Before diagnosing yourself with low self-esteem, make sure you're not surrounded by assholes."

The words hit Adrian deep. For the first time in a very long time, she was given a different perspective. With so many people constantly giving her a hard time, be it family or her peers, her mind had gotten used to being treated that way. The negativity had become her reality. The girl was at a loss for words when the smell of the burning ciggie distracted her. Jane was now holding it close to her face.

"Just a few drags," Jane insisted. "If it's not your cup of tea, we'll just head into the mall and get some ice cream."

Adrian cautiously held it between her index and middle finger. She noticed her fingers shaking while doing so. Jane lightly held them, much to Adrian's surprise.

"Now put the butt in your mouth, inhale like you're taking in air, then let it out," Jane instructed.

Adrian was already feeling the jitters from the delicate touch of Jane's fingers. She made an effort to focus on the burning stick that was emitting bothersome smoke into her eyes. She rubbed her eyes before placing it between her teeth and letting her lips rest on them. She inhaled as instructed, but the moment that happened, an abrupt strain hit her throat, causing her to cough.

"Amateur," Jane laughed, punching her shoulder. "It takes a while to get used to it. Hand it over, kid, and another might actually kill you."

Adrian refused. Having coughed out air on the first attempt, she was extra careful on the next few attempts. The coughs didn't stop, but they lessened.

"Maybe I'll get better with practice." Adrian swallowed.

"Na uh!" Jane stated. "That's probably the last time I'm seen you have that. Come on. Since you're a sport, I'm buying you chocolate. Double scoops."

Adrian felt a wave of comfort when Jane put her arm

around her shoulder.

"Make it triple." Adrian smiled.

"Now we're talking. Take that low self-esteem! You can't stop us today!"

Both the girls laughed, making their way into the mall. Adrian noticed some peering eyes from onlookers, but this time, she didn't care. What she needed was there.

What Adrian couldn't find at home or at school in terms of love and companionship, she found in Jane. One night, while staring at the stars, Adrian let out the most honest confession in a long time.

"It's getting late," Jane pointed out. "Aren't you gonna prep for home?"

"You are home."

Jane blushed, probably the first time Adrian ever managed to do that, and both held hands. The girl didn't want to deny it any further, she was in love with her best friend.

Countless times, Adrian stared at herself in the mirror, practicing and creating made up scenarios on how she was going to tell her. Keeping it in for so long just seemed to make it worse. She enjoyed having this secret, but now the urge was growing stronger by the day.

"Jane, this isn't easy, but… I love you," she whispered

to her reflection. "No, no. Thats too direct. Hey Jane, I'd like to talk to you about something. Nah, thats not right either."

"Hurry up in there!" said an angry tone.

Adrian quickly turned the tap and splashed water over her face. She walked out to find her father standing.

"This is the fourth time this week you've been in there, taking this long." he pointed out. "Something I should know about?"

Adrian felt a chill down her spine when her father crossed her arms.

"No, just a little tired because of too much homework."

With that, she took her leave. Her parents always wanted inside details regarding what was going on with her when it came to her health. This constant helicopter parenting escalated when she hit puberty. Something about her appearance kept bothering them all the more. Adrian never entertained the thought any further. She hated being reminded that, for some reason, she was an outsider.

After having pranked one of the 'meanies' from their class by placing a fake bouncing snake into her bag, they went off to their usual secret hideout, which was an abandoned cabin far off in the woods. The girls had found out about it when venturing as far away from the little town. If there was one thing that would both impress and annoy Adrian, it was Jane's never ending adventurous spirit.

Regardless of whether it was going to the mall or just dawdling at school, there was always something new to discover. The girls had managed to sneak into the principal's office, reach the mall's high roof, and caught one of their teachers smooching with her secret boyfriend at a park. The abandoned cabin was not something Adrian considered 'cool', but it always made Jane happy.

"Seriously, why are you so obsessed with coming here?" Adrian asked. "It's so dull and boring."

"It could be haunted and filled with spooky ghosts," Jane said. "Imagine Adrian. Right now. At this very moment, while you and I look behind these creaking doors and broken windows, spirits roam around us, waiting to share their wisdom."

"Or maybe they just want to possess us and use our bodies as vessels. Putting it out there, not interested."

Just as Adrian took her first step, her foot immediately fell through the creaking wood, causing both to panic.

"My foot!" Adrian gasped.

"Hang on! Hang on!" Jane rushed.

Jane leaned down and carefully held her friend's leg, trying to slowly pull it out. Even the slightest effort made

Adrian wince in pain.

"It stuck." Adrian groaned.

"Just put a little more effort, and it'll pop right out. On the count of three."

Jane yanked the leg right on one. Both fell back against the wall.

"Seriously?" Adrian sighed. "That's the last time we're doing maths together."

"Well, at least the physics of it all certainly helped."

The argument would've lasted longer had it not been for the creaking door. Both the girls froze in horror as the dark wooden door opened on its own, and from it appeared the most frightening thing yet: a mouse.

Usually, Jane was always ahead of Adrian when it came to running, but for the first time, both were screaming and running alongside one another. They must've outrun their usual distance, leaving behind the cabin. It wasn't until a few minutes later that they stopped and took a breath. When their eyes met, they laughed.

"Never again?" Adrian asked.

"Never."

They walked back towards their town when Adrian noticed something that made her stop immediately.

"Another mouse?" Jane panicked.

"No... that," Adrian said, pointing at the railway tracks ahead.

Jane stared confused.

"I don't understand."

Adrian started shaking as the memory came flashing back at her.

"There was a man..." she whispered. "He... was a bad person..."

Tears were already running down her cheeks.

"Hey, hey. It's okay," Jane insisted. "Close your eyes for me."

"What?"

"Trust me."

Adrian did as ask. She felt Jane's palms slowly pull her towards the track.

"I just told you-"

"Adrian, just focus on the sound of my voice and breathe."

The shaking increased, but Adrian followed her friend's instructions. Jane kept talking to her in a soothing voice. Despite her reservations, Adrian kept walking. She felt the steel beneath her feet, then stones, the other track, and then more earth.

"Open them."

Adrian turned to see that she had crossed the track. More tears followed. Jane held her face.

"As long as I am around, you don't have to be scared."

Whether it was instinct or desire, Adrian leaned ahead and kissed her friend on the lips. Jane pulled away immediately.

"I'm sorry!" Adrian gasped. "It was an accident."

The damage had already been done. Jane started stepping further away. Both looked at each other.

"No," was all Jane said before running off.

Adrian sat there crying. Life had played another one of its cruel tricks. She didn't even care that a dark cloud was starting to form, hinting at an upcoming storm.

The girl was used to being shouted at, being called names, and getting hit in the face now and then. What she was never used to was silence. Jane refused to speak, let alone interact with Adrian, for the next few weeks. There was something even more painful about her best friend not even wanting to look at her anymore. She would walk into class, sit on another chair and keep Adrian as distanced as possible.

Never before had Adrian felt so alone. She hated herself for doing what she did. Perhaps if she kept her feelings to herself, she would still have Jane around. Yet, not matter how much she thought back to what happened, she couldn't hold it in anymore. It was damned if she did, damned if she didn't.

During recess, Adrian rushed to Jane in the hopes of talking, but her hand was smacked away.

"Please, Adrian," Jane snapped. "I'd appreciate it if you respected my boundaries."

With that, the girl went off. Adrian realized that the last few months were simply a short-lived fantasy. Now, she had gone full circle and was back to being the sole loner. The joke on everyone's tongue.

Finals were around the corner, and it was the only thing that Adrian could focus on to distract herself. Jane would keep crossing her mind, but Adrian remained steadfast. It wasn't easy, and with each passing day, it got worse, but the girl just didn't want to give up. Her act of revealing her secret seemed to have opened up a sense of resilience that she wasn't familiar with. Her eyes were glued to the textbooks and the answer sheets. Even her family was surprised to see her not stepping out of her room.

The parents were able to put two and two together, considering her friend wasn't present as much, but that's how far they went in their contribution. They kept their fights to a minimum for the sake of their children, all of whom were locked in study mode.

The finals were going to play a big role in Adrian's life, or as many around her would say. This was her chance to either move to a new bog city in Taiwan or move abroad. Her father had shot the chances for the latter, stating that he had no money to fund her. From the sound of his voice, he probably just didn't want to.

Adrian was adamant now about getting out of this town. The one reason that had given her hope now was gone. Jane herself mentioned how she intended to leave the place, so in a matter of months, both would be on their different paths in life. Adrian just wished their goodbye could've happened.

The exams were a breeze for Adrian. She noticed plenty of her peers shivering with fear. Some even rushed to the bathroom to vomit. Others just broke down crying, unable to move. Yet, no one actually ran off. Everyone still gave their papers. Their parents wouldn't take it well if they came to know that their child didn't produce results.

Adrian walked out of her school as the breeze blew across her face. In the distance, she noticed Jane talking to a few people. She couldn't believe her eyes when she realized it was the mean bullies they would prank on. Had her friend betrayed them?

Jane noticed her staring and walked off. Some of the bullies noticed Adrian looking and laughed. Having already been through enough, Adrian went off in her own direction. Rather than take the bus like everyone else, she decided to walk home. It surprised her when she felt a tap on her shoulder. She turned around to face a boy in her class named Choi.

Choi was a strange one in the class. He'd either be goggling along with the meanies or just buried in his books. It was hard to tell whether he was just joining in for the sake of having some fun or he didn't really care. The question was, why was he trying to talk to Adrian?

"How was your exam?" he asked eagerly.

"Fine," Adrian replied. The awkwardness in her tone was blatantly obvious.

"Mine too. Listen, I know we don't talk much-"

"We don't talk at all."

Choi let out a nervous laugh. This was clearly not his element.

"I was wondering if you'd like to join me and a few friends at the lake today."

It took a moment for Adrian to realize that the boy had just asked if she wanted to hang out with him.

"Why?" was the first thing that came out of her mouth.

"Well, it's the last exam and only a week more with the school. After this, everyone goes to university-I"

"Why are you asking me to hang out with you guys? You've been jerks since day one."

A wave of guilt and sympathy came over Choi's face.

"Listen, I'm really sorry about that," he admitted. "I was a jerk, and so were plenty of others. But with it being the last day, I'd rather not have all of us have bad memories of each other."

"One nice time doesn't make up for years of being a jerk."

"You're right. It doesn't. But Jane told me."

"Jane?" Adrian gasped.

"Yeah. I figured she's a bit upset about how we've all been to you both. She knocked some sense into us. Listen, you have every right to say no. I'll completely understand."

Had Jane been actually speaking good on her behalf? Endless possibilities went rushing through Adrian's mind. Even though they weren't talking, Jane still made an effort to let the meanies know they did her wrong. Maybe she still cared about her after all.

"Well, since it's gonna take you a bit to decide," Choi continued, "We'll be there the day after tomorrow, past sunset.

Make sure to wear something swimming oriented."

With that, he took off. Adrian walked away pretending as if it were just another casual conversation, but her mind raced with questions. She contemplated the possibility of going, but after giving it plenty of thought, Adrian knew there would only be one reason for her to go there. Jane.

Adrian kept herself busy for the next day, hoping to sideline potential outcomes in her mind. It was a lot easier to keep herself distracted when she had exams happening, but now, with academics done and dusted, all she could do was wonder if Jane was ready to make amends. Was she inviting her to the lake with the others to patch up? Was Choi just being a prankster and trying to make a joke of her when she arrived?

The possibility of being ridiculed frightened the poor girl because, unlike before, she didn't have someone protecting her. She had garnered partial confidence, but that was easier to do with Jane around. Being on her own reminded her a bit of harsh truths, and she felt it was better to be safe than sorry. Yet, with each passing hour, the urge grew. She wanted to go to the lake and find out what Jane was doing there.

At the dinner table, everyone ate quietly, as was the rule. The siblings knew that it was best to eat silently rather than encourage any conversation, considering how on edge their parents were that day. Another argument occurred, and it was only a matter of time before the spark would fuel the fire.

Adrian ate a little and mentioned that she was going to be staying late at school to assist a teacher. Telling them about the lake was a sure shot at being told to stay home.

"For how long?" her father grumbled.

"It could stretch to very long, depending on how much work the teachers have."

"Isn't term over now?" Her mother inquired. "What could they possibly need now?"

Adrian noticed her siblings eyeing her curiously. Did they see through her bluff already?

"It's common for teachers to do that," Lu chimed in, much to Adrian's surprise. "Even I was made to do that last year."

Adrian couldn't believe her ears. Was her sister finally coming around? That was two twists within two days already. She had hoped for more acknowledgment from her sister, but the girl went back to her food.

"Alright," her father huffed. "Don't be gone too long. These teachers can do their work on their own. Lazy fools are all they're being."

With that, he deliberately tossed his plate away from him, letting it clatter all over the table. Adrian's mother glared at him as he walked out the door for his usual stroll. The other siblings quickly cleaned their plates and washed them. Adrian following along, and everyone parted ways. The fight was bound to happen sooner or later.

Adrian went to her room and found herself replaying the moment at the tracks. It hurt her to see her friend react the way she did, but she understood why Jane chose to do that. Maybe if it were someone else, the reaction could have been much uglier. She couldn't discard the fact that the last few months had been the best ones off her life, and that meant something. If there was a chance of making things right, then Adrian had to be there.

Tomorrow finally came along, and Adrian was hinted a reminder from Choi was nodded on his way out. Adrian stayed behind at the library. She had seen no sign of Jane that day. It was strange, considering that it was the last day, and everyone was mostly present. The students enjoyed themselves by throwing water balloons and ink on one another. Adrian hated those games because it was hard to tell whether they were tossing those things at her out of meaningless joy or meanness. That didn't spare her from a few spills of water and color. Hair was wet, and she hid herself in the library till the sun slowly started to move its way from the sky.

Adrian was familiar with where the lake was, but she never quite liked going there. It was always something of a risk if you were on your own because either a couple would be smooching about, or some creepy guy or group would start tailing you. Luckily, since most of the students went together as groups usually around this time, they didn't have to worry about unwanted company.

Adrian went there a little earlier, because she preferred having some sunlight to guide her. Like most of the entertainment spots of the little town, this lake was a bit far. If anyone went further than the lake, it was likely that they were heading for the dock. Adrian dreamed of going there, jumping on a ship and sailing off to the horizon, but like many things, it seemed like a far-fetched dream.

The lake was within sight, and Adrian could already see plenty of familiar faces. Most of the crowd consisted of the usual class mates, some juniors as well. They had liquor bottles in their hand, and in the corner, some were busy cooking up food. Some prying eyes followed her, but most preferred being in their own company. Adrian felt a bit of relief from that. Someone handed her a bottle without even looking in her direction. Adrian took it and continued to look around.

There was no sign of Jane anywhere, and that worried Adrian all the more. Chang appeared in the distance and waved. From the look on his face, it surprised him more that Adrian came along. He gestured for her to join him. The boy was sitting on a large wooden branch that was cut in a manner to make it look like a bench. Adrian walked over.

"Everyone," he said. "You all remember Adrian."

"You came?" a surprised voice said.

"Ssshhh!" Chang snapped. "Be nice."

Adrian sat down awkwardly and sipped her drink to look busy. The conversations continued, and she simply nodded while pretending to sip more of the drink.

It started to get dark around the time when Adrian contemplated leaving. The moment she stood up was the moment she spotted Jane arriving. She couldn't believe her eyes when she noticed one of the mean bullies had his arm around her. They walked to their corner, giggling about something. Jane and Adrian's eyes met, but the former looked away disappointed. The latter felt her heart sink.

"Are you leaving?" Chang asked.

"No, I... I think I'm going to have another one of these," she replied, tapping her bottle.

"Alright! Thats the spirit!" one of the kids cheered.

Adrian strolled around for a bit and noticed Jane going for the cooler box. This was her chance. She reached Jane much faster than she expected to. The girl turned and was taken aback by Adrian in front of her.

"What do you want?" was the first thing Jane said. The tone it came with already upsets Adrian.

"Can we talk, please?"

"We are talking."

Adrian looked around to see no one paying attention to them.

"Somewhere alone."

Jane looked uncomfortable with that suggestion.

"No," she said immediately. "I'm sticking with Ling over there."

Adrian realized that Ling was the fellow she had walked in with. His haircut made him difficult to recognize. His long-haired ponytail was replaced with a crew cut. He was among the mean bullies.

"Why are you hanging out with him?" Adrian asked. "A month back, he was taking verbal jabs at us."

"At you."

Adrian felt the situation get worse at the moment. This was not her friend from before. Something had changed.

"Why are you being like this?" was all the girl could ask. "I thought we were friends."

"We were. We are not anymore."

Jane took a bottle of liquor and made her way back. Adrian made no attempt to plead. Whatever urge there was to make amends was now tarnished.

It had only been a few moments of interaction, but

Jane displayed this finality that was bound to stay for a very long time. Adrian could not wrap her head around it and decided that it was time to go back home.

"Hey, everybody!" someone cheered. "Time for testimonials."

Before Adrian could even react, the entire group got together into a huddle, and she was pulled along. Food and drinks were distributed while the sky turned dark. Hints of a few stars were already showing, and the chilly breeze made its presence clear. Adrian was glad she dressed warmly. She had no intention of getting into the water like the others had.

Everyone seemed to have brought notes along with them. Friends and peers were dishing compliments to one another, which felt oddly out of place for Adrian. She was generally the butt of everyone's joke, but everyone had a tendency of teasing one another or taking a jab at someone else's expense. The fact that some of them were getting tear eyed when saying nice things gave Adrian a completely different perception of her peers. Some, in fact, started crying, boys included, because it was difficult for them to accept that the good times were indeed coming to an end, and everyone as going their separate ways.

Adrian started to wonder if there was a possibility that the others might add a kind word for her. They might even apologize for being mean the whole time. It felt too good to be true, and seeing how everyone was starting to get emotional, she felt it was best to leave. She tried to glance at Jane one last time, but she had her head leaning on Ling's shoulder. That was enough for Adrian to slowly start getting up.

"Hey, where are you going?" Ling asked. "We're just about to come to you."

Adrian looked around, confused. They were passing a large poster in her direction. It was rolled up, so Adrian had to wait a moment before she could see what was written on it.

"This is a goodbye present from everyone here," Ling said, grinning. "Something to remember us by."

Once the poster reached her, Adrian unrolled the paper. As she did, a sound of muffled giggles echoed. The others were struggling to fight back their laugh. It was not until she finally saw what was on the poster that everything came together.

It was a picture of her head, badly placed on a body that was an amalgamation of a man's and woman's parts. Its oddity reflected the opinion they had of her. They went through the trouble of placing her class photo and then adding it to something that looked ridiculously ugly. The muffled and held-back laughs now came rushing out.

Adrian looked to see everyone laughing at her. Some of them were having a hysterical reaction and made no effort to hold themselves together.

"Like I said," Ling giggled. "Something I'm sure you won't forget."

"Aww, look," a voice pointed out. "She's' about to cry."

Had that person not highlighted that maybe Adrian would have. It was as if someone had punched her hard in the gut. The sight of Jane smiling along to the others made it worse. Adrian felt something break inside, and a seething anger began to manifest in her mind. Her eyes shot straight to Ling.

"What's the matter Tranny?" he spat. "Don't like your present?"

Adrian stepped ahead and swung her fist right into his face. She had never displayed physical force before. Now she saw that there was plenty of muscle on her. Ling went flying back, falling hard to the ground. The laughter ceased, and everyone went silent.

The faces looked first at Ling, who was bleeding out of his nose and mouth. Then they looked to Adrian, who stood there, as surprised as everyone. For her, it was as if something that had been waiting to come out for a very long time. Now it had, and there were consequences.

"What the hell!" Ling sobbed as blood spluttered out

of his mouth. "Do something!"

Before Adrian could react, she noticed Jane running off before the entire mob came straight at her. Out of instinct, the girl managed to knock down three more of the boys, but the numbers would overwhelm her. She covered her face when the kicks came her way, but it did little to help. The punches and clawing began bruising her body and tearing her clothes.

Adrian would have been knocked unconscious had Chang not dived in and covered her with his body. He took plenty of hits in the process.

"What the hell!" someone shouted at him.

"Let it go!" he pleaded. "We're all even now."

The group stepped back. Everyone was heaving for breath. Something about Adrian garnered their attention. They stood at her awkwardly. Adrian struggled to her feet with the help of Chang, but even he let her arm go when he noticed something.

Adrian noticed a considerable chunk of her clothing had been ruined, and with that, a considerable chunk of her body was showing.

"She… she really is a tranny." Someone said.

There was more fear than mockery in that tone. Adrian looked to see their faces and felt her eyes well up. She noticed Jane even staring dumbfounded. The girl was unable to bear it anymore and ran off. Branches struck her face, rude words were called out behind her, and she tripped and hurt herself, but she never stopped running. The shame and humiliation were too much to bear.

Adrian knew that at one moment, she was running away from the lake, and the next, she was falling down in her house. Her crash alerted the entire house. Her family came rushing to the door and were taken aback by her appearance.

"What in the world happened?" her father growled. Something about the anger in his tone infuriated Adrian.

"Why don't you put two and two together and figure it out!" Adrian spat back.

Her siblings gasped, along with her mother. Her father was taken aback but immediately switched to anger.

"You dare speak to me that way!" he shouted, making his children cower behind. "I am your father! You are to talk to me with respect."

Adrian felt the fire come out of her again. Some form of adrenaline had kicked in, and she wasn't scared of the patriarch anymore. She stood tall and looked at her father in the eye.

"Respect? She repeated. "What do you know about that word? To you, respect is about having things done your way. If anyone even so resists, its only moments before you shout and hurt us to make your point. We're are your family. I am your daughter. It's not a plaything. I walk in looking like… this! And you don't even step forward to hold me in your arms. None of you do!"

A silence fell in the house. Whatever that was left unsaid came out at that very moment.

"You're not a parent. None of you are a family." Adrian sobbed. "You're all just bullies. You hurt each other. And you've hurt me. Everyone has."

Adrian's eyes caught her father's hand turning into a fist. That infuriated her more. She noticed his face was that of worry rather than intimidation. He was scared, but he was still going to assert his authority. The moment he took a step forward, Adrian was ready.

"You will be punished for your attitude!" he said, forcing a growl.

The next thing Adrian knew was that she had punched her father to the ground, just like she did with Chang. The attack by the mob made her all the more defensive. She watched as everyone rushed to her father to see if he was okay. Then they looked back at her with fear.

"What have you done?" Lao whispered.

Adrian looked at her mother, surprised at her very own reaction.

"Leave." was all her mother said.

The tears rolled, but the girl was not going to show weakness. Not now. Not ever. She rushed to her room, packed her things, and left from the window. She ran far out to the one place that she knew would be her last resort. The docks. Adrian always imagined looking back at her house on the day she would leave, but she never looked back. This place was not her home. Her life had ended in that town, and now she had to start another.

Chapter Three

Adrian stared at the stars above. Sounds of sirens and shouting hooligans echoed even at that late hour. She puffed her cigarette and took a deep breath. The day had been long and more tiring than expected. She had just finished her shift at the strip club and had to get Jimmy, her bouncer, to fend off another creep.

"Thats the fifth one this week," Jimmy complained, cracking his fingers.

"At least I keep you busy." she teased.

The six-foot titan smiled and nodded. He enjoyed whacking a few weirdos now and then. Both of them were glad the fella didn't have a gun.

Adrian's eyes fell on a couple that were kissing on their balcony. They had been talking over drinks, and now the kissing had begun. There was something endearing about that sight, and she smiled. Taking in the last puff, she crushed the cigarette butt underneath her heel.

"Hey! Miss Tashia Thailand!" she heard her manager shout from the door. "Get down here!"

The girl sighed and rubbed her eyes. That fat moron was ready for another shouting match. Adrian knew she didn't have the energy, so it was best to let the tiny man have his way. She walked downstairs, passing by the makeup room where all the other strippers were either smoking or fixing themselves up in the mirror.

"Hey, Tashia," one of them said. "Wanna go out for drinks?"

"Not tonight, Bella," she replied. "Gonna call it in early."

"Like a true grandmother."

The two shared a laugh before the manager started shouting.

"Yes, Enrique!" she's coming, Bella yelled. "Don't piss him off any further. The cops paid a visit again."

"Did he tell you to say that?" Adrian sighed.

"Nope. I promised him a lap dance just to go easy on Enrique. He showed me his ring."

A couple of oohs and aah's echoed in the makeup room.

"A dedicated husband at a whorehouse," one chimed. "What a predicament."

Adrian knocked on the already tattered door. There was a bullet hole near the knock where she placed her fingers and pushed. As usual, the balding jerk had his hands pressed in his face. The room reeked of alcohol and cigarettes. A stench Adrian could never get used to. She noticed a bottle of vodka on the desk and reached for it. The smell was one thing, but the taste was worth it.

"Speak my King," Adrian scoffed, gulping a solid amount.

Enrique rubbed his eyes and looked at her, resting his scarred cheek on a relaxed fist.

"Tashia," he groaned. "How long have you been working here?"

"2 years, six months, and eleven days. But whose counting right."

"You were bartending here for the first year."

"And cleaning toilets."

"Yes, yes, and cleaning toilets. Tell me, what exactly do we do here?"

Adrian eyed him for a moment. The silence that followed was filled with boredom.

"We give our customers a hot and sexy time."

"Correct, so… why is it that when you're giving private lap dances, I find customers leaving with broken bones? You and Jimmy got something going on?"

"That macho of a man? I'd be one lucky woman to have him carry me around."

"Jesus woman! Can you, for once, be professional? Just once, God dammit!"

"Enrique! It's difficult doing any of that in this line of work! I take my clothes off for a living. These creeps here get a hard on, and now you expect me to just take their crap! I'm a dancer! Not their God damn plaything."

"We give a service here. It's called escapism. Their TVs and phones can never come close to the real deal we give. Anyone can look up porn. But here, we're physically present. When that happens, these 'creeps' pay a shit ton of money. They don't care about their savings, they don't know if their wives need money for groceries later. They just wanna see some tits and ass. Let them have this!"

Adrian leaned back in her chair and crossed her arms.

"Sometimes Enrique," she said. "I wish you were me. Just so you know what it's like."

Enrique leaned closer with his fist pressed on the table.

"Tashia, I couldn't be more grateful that I am not. So, thank you for being an example of why I should thank the Almighty."

"You're a fucking asshole!" Adrian snapped, taking her leave.

"Stop having Jimmy hurt the customers, Tashia," he called out, bored.

"Screw you! And that wig isn't fooling anybody."

The girls noticed Adrian storm out. She didn't even bother picking up her purse. Bella was quick to act. Someone tossed her the purse, and she was out the door.

"Tashia!" she called out. It took a moment for her to see it was raining hard. "Your purse! And at least take an umbrella."

Adrian stopped for a moment and let the water fall down on her hard. It was no secret that the manager was an asshole. She just hated it when he would get under her skin. If she had more energy, she would've finished him with an angry rant. The raindrops ceased immediately, and Adrian turned to see a smiling Bella holding her umbrella.

"You okay, babe?" she asked.

Adrian fought back her tears and followed her to the sidewalk, lighting up another cigarette.

"Enrique worked his charm, huh?" Bella asked.

"It was very effective." Adrian spat.

They both stood there in silence as one of them finished her cigarette.

"He's a scumbag Tashia," Bella consoled.

"And I work for a scumbag, I guess that says a lot about me."

"People like us don't really get to have a choice in this. We make do with what we got."

"Thank you for the pepper talk, Bella. I gotta get going before I reconsider and tear that fucker's hair off."

"It's pep talk, Tashia."

"Whatever!" snapped before snatching the purse.

"Hey! What about the umbrella?"

Adrian said nothing. She simply waved her hand and kept walking. Even though some cars passed by, there weren't too many. Adrian didn't mind a long walk back to her apartment. A few streets down, she decided to take off her heels and began to walk barefoot. the concrete sidewalk pestered her toughened feet, but it was the flow of the rain that she enjoyed. Some strangers stared at her as she went by, one of them whistled. Just another Tuesday night for Tashia Thailand.

Adrian never quite liked the name, but her line of work didn't take too kindly to something that generic. Everybody thought she was Chinese, but when she said Thailand, the strippers at the club immediately took a shine to it, and added a Russian name.

"This'll fascinate the customers." Enrique insisted.

The only fascination the customers had was around her breasts and buttocks. They couldn't care less about where she was from or what her favorite color was. There were occasions when someone would get a closer look and realize what she actually was, they'd get upset.

"What the fuck!" one gasped. "I didn't want a fucking tranny."

That was Jimmy's queue to walk in. It had become something of a pattern that Adrian was numb to their anger. The first time, though, she threw the man's drink back at him and cried for three days.

Coming to America was a dream for the now much older Adrian. It had been seven years since she landed in the land of opportunity, but the only opportunity she could find was either stripping or pimping. Her dreamland was nothing more than a facade of glitz and glory. They had a good front of progress and beauty, but the underbelly was the real backbone of their economy. In other words, America wasn't as different from her home. The good thing was that her Adrian no longer had a family to be worried or scared of. Those fears were replaced by bigots, homophobes, and drunkards now.

Adrian stumbled on a step when a flashlight hit her eyes. She turned to see a police car pull around, much to her horror. Those men in uniform were nothing but trouble. Adrian remained still till she noticed something familiar about his face.

"Tashia, right," the officer said. "Officer Jenkins. I spoke with Enrique this evening."

"Please, officer," Adrian pleaded. "I don't want any trouble."

"I don't either, so cooperate and get in the car. Now."

Adrian had been around long enough to know that when the coppers gave an instruction, it was best to follow it through. There were countless ugly stories about what would happen if you pissed off the men in blue. Being a stripper herself, there was no way anyone was going to pity her if she ended up dead the next day in a ditch.

"Okay, officer." Adrian gulped. "Just please don't hurt me."

Jenkins opened the back door and gestured at her. The girl quickly got in and started recalling every prayer she was taught as a child. She observed Jenkins walk over to the driver's seat.

"Seatbelts," he instructed. Adrian did as ask to do.

The car drove in silence for quite some time. Adrian couldn't hold back her fear any further.

"Please, officer!" she pleaded. "I haven't done anything wrong! I swear I abide by all the laws! I even pay my taxes-"

"Hey, relax," he reassured her. "You're not under arrest." Adrian blinked. Her eyes looked to the rearview mirror, where she caught his glance.

"I'm just getting you home safe and sound."

"Why?"

The question amused the officer.

"I'm wearing a uniform, Tashia," he said. "It's my job."

Adrian still couldn't put two and two together.

"I was at the club sometime back," he explained. "Apparently, one of the customers complained that the place was a front for smuggling drugs. It didn't take me long to figure out that he was given the 'treatment' from that buffoon Jimmy. Enrique told me that most of your clients tend to have a bit of trouble."

Jenkins' eyes met hers in the rearview mirror.

"No judgement here Tashia." he said. "It's a dirty business, and a lot happens there. There is a reason why they put up so many locked doors and curtains there. I'm pretty sure it's not for decor. Enrique is not that bright, to be honest.

"At least we can agree on something." Adrian thought.

"But that aside, I'm a little worried for your safety. One of the punks got messed up pretty badly and hinted at giving you more trouble. So, as a precaution, I'm getting you home.

I insist that you stay indoors for some time. Besides, there's plenty happening in the city, so better safe than sorry."

Adrian's heart sank. It was comforting that there were still good men out there willing to keep her safe. But it was just as frightening to know that another one was lurking in the shadows, ready to strike.

"You got some friend who you can stay over at?" he asked.

"I'll bunk in with Jimmy. Plenty of us girls go to him when trouble comes around."

"Alright then. Once you're home, pack your things and come straight down. I'm not taking chances tonight."

They arrived at Adrian's shanty apartment. The place was a wreck from the foundation to the shattered roof. Plenty of windows were cracked, and the walls were filled with homophobic slurs. Even Jenkins looked surprised at the condition of the place.

"Welcome to my world." Adrian sighed.

"It's not going to be for the next couple of weeks," he said. "Hurry it up."

Adrian rushed in. Luckily her apartment was on the first floor, so she didn't have to climb so many stairs. Gathering her essentials along with the many dresses, Adrian hurried her way out. Jenkins was quick to start the car and drive off.

"Listen up," he said. "I shouldn't have to tell you much, but it's best to keep yourself busy elsewhere. Now, before you jump to not being able to find work, please look into this."

Jenkins passed her a paper. Adrian took it and read.

"Volunteers wanted for… pride parade?" she asked, confused. "Do they even pay?"

"I'll talk to a friend who can give you something under the table. But this ought to keep you busy till those punk calms down and pisses off elsewhere. I'll have someone keep an eye on him."

Adrian knew a bit about the pride parade, but only in bits and pieces. A lot of pink and bright colors, along with people marching with joy. She never liked big crowds but didn't quite see what other option she had. No one was going to let her in to clean the dishes or even clean the bathrooms. She had to find ways to make cash elsewhere. Joining another strip club would only garner Enrique's wrath. They didn't like their assets being somewhere else. Shootouts and street fights would break out over things like these.

"Officer," Adrian said. "Are you sure this place will help?"

The man smiled. It was then that she noticed how good looking he was. His charm was hidden behind a facade of toughness.

"In more ways than you can even imagine." he nodded.

Coming around the curve, he dropped Adrian to Jimmy's hideout. The usual onlookers ran off when noticing the siren. Adrian made her way out of the car. She turned around to look at Officer Jenkins once more.

"Thank you," was the best she could muster.

"You sleep well," he replied. "Stay out of trouble."

She watched him drive off into the night. The rain was still pouring. Adrian moved to the door and opened it. Jimmy never locked his place. The robbers were more scared of him and his blood hound, Zeus.

Adrian jumped at the sight of the Rottweiler coming up to her out of the blue and licking her face.

"Oh, stop, stop." she giggled. "Hey, Jimmy. Did you feed Zeus yet?"

"Yes," came a grunting sound. He was probably lifting weights. "Don't let his sad eyes fool you."

"Too late. They won me already."

Adrian wasn't the only woman in that place that night. She was surprised to see another girl, no older than sixteen, sitting on a chair, applying alcohol to her wound. She stopped the moment she noticed Adrian walk in.

"Tashia, Jezebel. Jezebel, Tashia." Jimmy clarified, grunting more as he did another deadlift.

"You too, huh?" Adrian asked.

The girl remained quiet. She kept looking back at Jimmy, who was too focused on his workout.

"Here, let me help you."

Adrian walked over to the girl. She picked up the gauze, dipped some whiskey on it, and leaned forward. The girl started shivering more. Adrian reached out her hand and patted gently on her short red hair.

"Hey, it's okay," she whispered. "You're safe here."

The girl began whimpering and instead pressed her head into Adrian's chest. The whimpers turned to sobs. Adrian placed down the gauze and embraced her tight. She could feel her own tears almost sprouting.

"The pimp was overdoing it," Jimmy said, putting down the weights. "Had he continued, she'd be in the hospital.

"Thank you, Jimmy," Adrian said. "Is the spare bed fixed?"

"No. The assholes didn't show up today. I got three mattresses that are solid."

Adrian helped the girl to her room and pressed the gauze on her bruised cheek under the lamplight. After some wincing, she finally came around.

"What's your name?" Adrian asked.

"Jezebel."

"Your real name."

"Clara."

"What a beautiful name." Adrian helped the girl with the blankets and a pillow before going to her mattress. She stared at the flyer Jenkins gave her and began to think a lot about what he meant. She was going to call the number first thing tomorrow.

Lightning struck in the distance, but luckily, thunder didn't make a lot of noise. Adrian stared out of the window with a heavy heart and felt her eyes close. Perhaps, like always, her dreams would take her to a happier place.

Adrian was back home. In the distance was her old house with her family standing there. They gestured for her to come, but she was unable to move. The house kept moving further away. A loud siren blared, and Adrian turned around to see the ship about to set sail.

"Come home, Adrian!" she heard her mother say.

The house and her family were too far, and Adrian felt the need to run away from them. She dashed for the blaring ship only to see that she could barely move. Her legs were glued to the grown, and her arms would hardly sway. The ship began to sail away, and within moments, it disappeared into the horizon. Her family shifted into large shadows that began to encompass the sky. They loomed over her and charged, screaming.

"Come home!" they roared in unison.

Adrian woke up in a cold sweat. Her sudden movement almost woke Clara. The girl shuffled on her mattress before almost getting up.

"It's okay," Adrian said quickly, catching her breath. "Just a bad dream. Go back to sleep."

The girl did as ask. Adrian got up and walked downstairs, where Jimmy sat looking out of the window.

"Can't sleep?" he asked, sensing her presence. His eyes remained glued to the rain outside.

"The sky is still pissing on us?" Adrian asked.

"I'll take that as a yes."

"For someone who isn't so smart, you're gifted in taking a hint."

"You sound like my caretaker from the orphanage. Jimmy, it's okay not to get the grades; just be sharp enough to read a room. Truth be told, I still mess up many times."

"You're a fighter, Jimmy. I'm sure the ring gives enough hints to know what is going to happen next."

"It's a bit trickier at the club. Girls speak in funny ways."

Adrian giggled at that. It was no secret that all the strippers had a secret language to make sure Enrique or the customers didn't catch on what was being shared. That was the certain guarantee of not getting into trouble.

"Don't worry big guy," Adrian mentioned, patting his shoulder. "You're not missing out on much. Is the puff-puff around?"

That managed to get Jimmy to turn around and look at her with concern.

"That is not good for you when you have it too many times." He stated.

Adrian was already checking through the drawers. Having been given a rude awakening and now having a not so bright fella telling her drugs were bad, we were starting to nag her nerves.

"It's just a few chunks, and then I'm done, Jimmy," she sighed. "You're reacting as if I'm already an addict."

Jimmy crossed his arms.

"Everyone thinks they are the inception." He said darkly. "It starts with a little amount, and then before you know it, you can't let it go."

Adrian blinked.

"I think you mean… exception."

Jimmy thought for a moment, scratching his head.

"Yeah, that." He said, somewhat lost.

"Jimmy, I'm an adult. I know how much I can take and when to stop. I'd appreciate it if you would respect my wishes. Read the room."

Jimmy wasn't pleased with that remark but gave in either way.

"Can never win an argument with a woman," he muttered.

"Neither could Einstein."

"Who?"

"Puff-Puff Jimmy."

The walking giant went over to a painting and pulled it to one side. He really was going the extra mile to keep the substances hidden. He moved the dial on the safe, more times than he should. It came as no surprise that he kept getting the combination wrong. After his seventh attempt, the safe finally opened. Adrian felt it was more luck than getting the code right. He reached in and tossed her a bag of marijuana. Adrian shook it, smelt it, and then felt it.

"Good quality," she admitted.

"If anyone asks, I-"

"Had nothing to do with it. My lips are sealed. You should get some sleep now."

"In some time."

The big guy again went back to his chair and stared out of the window. He was one of the very few people who could stare at a wall for fifteen minutes rather than scroll through his phone. Adrian never new how he could tolerate boredom. Maybe the fact he was such made it easy.

Adrian went up to the roof, picking up rolling paper and a lighter on the way. Much to her relief, it was only a light drizzle. There was a spot where Jimmy had placed multiple blocks on top of one another to make a giant square. Should it rain, she could stand underneath it. She looked at the structure and wondered how much time and effort went into it, even though it didn't serve a single purpose.

Jimmy had the rotten luck of being born in the wrong century. Maybe about some centuries back, he would have been worshipped as the ultimate warrior. In modern times, all people saw was a giant fool that made money in underground fights, and kept things calm in bars and clubs. Yet, unlike Adrian, he always seemed to enjoy doing such simple things. Despite being dealt a bad hand in life, he seemed to be content in the place he was in. Adrian wondered whether his lack of thinking skills contributed to that, or that he just didn't care.

"You're blessed, Jimmy," she whispered, having rolled and lit the joint. "You just don't know it yet. Maybe... you never will."

Adrian took a deep puff before staring out at the city lights. Cars and sirens still echoed, but they were much less in number. America was the kind of country where there was always someone or another who was still working. Adrian would notice building that had all of their lights off, but there would be one flicker in the building. She didn't have to guess that someone was probably working after hours. The work ethic here was unlike anything she had experienced before. People did work in Thailand; plenty of them would put their heart and soul into it, but Americans had something of an obsession with it.

The culture shock of the new word really took Adrian off guard when she landed in New York. She couldn't believe her eyes, when she saw the statue of liberty. Plenty of people around here stood in awe. They had been in the water for weeks without any trouble. Some were dreading the possibility of the ship sinking or a storm getting the better of them. Nothing happened. The pace of the travel was very slow. The longer it took, the more paranoid people became. Adrian didn't mingle much with the others. She couldn't. When she reached the dock, she was still in bad shape from the beating of the crowd.

It was some sympathetic stranger who took pity on her and provided her with a wash and some clothes, before letting her off into the ship. She wasn't allowed to go about, so she stayed in her room. It took some time for it to sink in that the man who was helping her did, in fact, have some motive. He would become the first sexual experience Adrian had. The more favors she did for him, the more he provided in exchange. Food, clothes, medicine, whatever she needed.

Adrian did feel used at first, but his kindness after fucking would make her second guess everything. The man had his requirements and gave her what she wanted. It's not like she had much other choice either. Plenty of people on the ship were no different than the ones she was leaving behind. It was like carrying her home with her. The prejudiced part of it. The man gave her security and would walk with her around in case she needed to.

He never shared his name, who he was, where he was from and what he was going to America for. He only requested that he be called Sir and nothing else. Weeks passed and she remained in his company. Adrian was never one to be social so both became accustomed to one another's company without having to say much. The oddity of it all was when the ship finally reached the dock. Adrian was expecting him to escort her out, but he never showed up. She waited in the cabin for hours and then worried someone would find her. Looking around the ship carefully, there was no sign of him. Realizing she was on her own, the girl took her chances and stepped on New York City, the city that never sleeps.

The first few weeks were the toughest, as Adrian could barely figure out the place. The skyscrapers shot far up to the sky, cars whizzed by like bullets and huge crowds were walking without stopping. She knew enough English to do the basic things, but no one seemed interested in talking. The nights were the scariest. Adrian would hide in alleyways, hoping no one would catch her.

One night, she felt some strangers hovering over her. She woke up to find two chefs staring at her. Both of them were Thai, as they spoke to her in their local dialect. One was a short, thin-mustached old man, and next to him was a tall fellow who Adrian assumed was his son.

"What're you doing here?" the old one asked.

Adrian quickly got up, but they stood in front of her against the wall, making it impossible for her to leave.

"Answer the question." The son insisted.

"I'm sorry," Adrian gulped as her legs shivered. "I don't have any place to go."

"We've heard that one many times," the son said. "Take your things and piss off. Or I'll smack you whore!"

"You'll do no such thing!" a voice cut through.

The father and son turned to see an elderly woman standing there.

"Mother," the boy said. "This isn't any of your business. This is a prostitute. She shouldn't be around our restaurant. We can get into plenty of trouble. I'm gonna call the cops."

"Did you just say no to me!" the woman snapped. She stepped closer to both the men, who now seemed out of their intimidating element. "This woman is hurt and hungry. She needs food. I want you two inside cooking a meal."

"My dear," the old man pleaded. "You know what happens when we bring strangers in our-"

The old lady shot a glance and that was the end of the discussion. Adrian had never seen authority being displayed like that. The woman was the same height as the man, but her presence was overwhelming. Her stern eyes looked to Adrian, and became kind.

"Come on child," she insisted, helping her up. "Let's get you out of those clothes and a meal. By God, this city has not been kind to you."

Adrian took a long final puff of her joint and smiled. It had been quite a while since she last thought of Yin. She was quite the woman. Flicking away the cigarette, she walked about the roof, letting the cold air enter her lungs. The more the air went into her system, the stronger the memory became. She found herself recollecting the moment when she was given a new set of clothes, ate a healthy meal, and slept on a warm bed. Taking another, she wiped a tear.

Yin was an amalgamation of a loving granny and a drill sergeant. For someone who wasn't an inch over 5 foot 4, her presence towered over everyone who worked there. The Thai restaurant was as generic as the others in the area, but what set it apart was Yin herself. She was the matriarch of the place, and everyone around knew. The competition was extra careful when they paid a visit for some help or to discuss certain matters. No one was spared form Yin's glare.

Yin, her husband, Ting and her son, Lee, were immigrants just like Adrian herself. They, too, had their fair share of troubles in the big apple. Perhaps that was why Yin took pity on Adrian. She knew the struggle and was willing to lend a helping hand. Her husband and son, however, were a different story.

Neither of the men hid their disdain for her. They looked at her with animosity, especially Lee. When Adrian was asked to work in the restaurant, Lee was quick to display his reservations.

"We don't let trannies work here!" he shouted. "They bring a bad omen wherever they go."

Yin, who was sipping her tea at the time, paused, placed her cup on the table, and stared at her son.

"Let me tell you some words, and listen to them well." She growled. "A person in need was outside our doorstep. This was life reminding us from where we started off to where we are now. You were too little to remember, but your father and I slogged and ate scraps. We made it a point to make sure you got the cleaner and bigger chunk of the meal. Everything we are now is through the help of the people of our community.

Now that I have taken in this girl to help around, she is a part of the house. You will treat her with respect and dignity. I raised you to be a man, not a bully. Not a bigot. A man! And the next time I hear the word 'tranny' from your tongue, I will walk the streets declaring that I have no son."

The silence that followed was deathly. Lee from that day on, didn't vent as much, but there was always some passive aggression when he interacted with Adrian. Ting was mostly silent, but he never displayed any interest.

Adrian started with washing dishes and cleaning up. Yin took out time and taught her to cook dishes Adrian had never heard of.

"Yankees love their burgers and hot dogs more than anything else," Yin instructed. "It has to be greasy and cheesy with some room for meat."

Adrian could never stand the sight of oil and spice leaking all over the buns. The size of those things was either tiny or huge.

"Madam Yin," Adrian gagged. "I think the Thai dishes are more to my liking."

"You're in America, child. People from around the world come here. You need to know every kind of dish possible if you want to make it in the restaurant business. In fact, I'd suggest you learn Espanol as soon as possible. Now press on the bun with that spatula."

Adrian was more horrified as tons of sauces oozed from the creation in front of her. The look on her face made Yin giggle, a rare occurrence.

"I think a strong stomach will also be necessary. But for now, let's try a more *desi* dish?"

"*Desi?*"

"It's a reference to people from the sub-continent. Ask that Pakistani Ahmed to come over from next door. He'll give us the needed recipes."

Despite the Ting and Lee, Adrian was happy being given shelter, food, and clothing. She was now working and made it a point to be good at it. Cleaning the bathroom was one of the most gag inducing parts of the job, and it was no secret that most of the crew gave her that job because they didn't want to do it. At times, Adrian felt she was there to clean up other people's mess. Her only lifeline was Yin, but the old lady couldn't always be around.

The customers were a mixed bag. Some seemed to notice Adiran's physical traits and felt uncomfortable, while others were oddly too kind and nice.

"You're a strong, brave woman for doing this," a white woman said to her. "You're an inspiration for your kind."

There was something odd to her compliments. She wasn't the only one. White people women in particular seemed keen on complimenting her, while others gave an uncomfortable. The ones who just wanted to order, eat and mind their own business were Adrian's favorite.

Dealing with an angry customer was another story. Adrian could tell that every now and then, some people stirred trouble just to avoid paying. 'The customer was always right' was bullshit in her opinion. Yet, despite the hurdles, Adrian continued head on. She was a student in a kind of school that gave her an education unlike any other. The real world.

However, her time at Ying's came to an end. Dealing with an angry customer that day, she faced a homophobic slur. It was enough to send her to the bathroom, where she cried till her eyes ached. To add more insult to injury, some of the cooks in the kitchen framed her for stealing money from the cashier. Had it not been for the secret camera that Ying placed in the cashier machine, Adrian would have time to prove herself innocent. No one took money, Paul, a long-haired blondie who had a knack for stirring trouble, simply took the money and placed it elsewhere. That was his last day at work.

Ying gathered everyone around and gave them a piece of her mind. As much as Adrian was grateful for her stance, she knew deep down inside that the time had come for her to leave. She had learned all that she needed to, and it was time to move on.

With a heavy heart, she relayed her feelings to the matriarch and handed in her resignation. It was the first time where she had a conversation where she had chosen to leave, and the other person sat and listened. Ying was visibly disappointed to see her leave but understood the girl's sentiment. Any place that served food was known to be a ground for ugly fights in the kitchen. Adrian didn't want to be an extra burden.

Packing up her things, she hugged Yin goodbye, bowed respectfully to Ting, and flipped off Lee on the way out. From then on, Adrian dabbled in one restaurant after another. She slogged through janitorial work and even walked the dog in the park. Yet, none of that helped garner enough money to have a roof over my head. The girl was close to finding herself back in the same cycle till she crossed Enrique.

Lightning struck in the far distance over the skyscrapers, but no thunder followed along. It was an odd sight that held its own unconventional beauty. Tall silhouettes, darkened sky, streams of many lights in different spots. The flash of lightning would smother them with blue and white for only a second.

These were the moments that would have Adrian think about how far she had come. She wasn't close to the ideal life that she imagined, but she wasn't stuck in the nightmare of home. New York wasn't exactly kind, but there were still plenty of good people helping her out. That is what gave her hope. Maybe she would never make it big, but at least she had a life of her own, and the city would always give moments of bliss to relieve her of the stress. This was now one of them, plus the joint had done its job.

Adrian felt her head become heavy and her thoughts. Sleep was making its way back, and she walked back to the comfort of the mattress. Resting her head on the pillow, she took one last look at the flyer and made up her mind. Change was the one thing that guaranteed a twist in her circumstances. If she wanted to break from the cycle of her usual line of work, she had to check out the pride meeting.

Since it was Jimmy's place, Arian woke up to the sun shining on her face. She had told the jock about getting curtains, but he would always forget. Considering that he preferred being downstairs most of the time, it didn't really make sense for him to buy things for people who would come and go. Adrian came downstairs to find Clara and Jimmy on the table. The former nibbled on her eggs as if she was scared of it, while the latter hogged one piece of bacon after another.

"Rise and shine!" Jimmy slobbered. "Don't talk with your mouth full." Adrian reminded him.

The buffoon quickly swallowed his whole chunk, not the first thing Adrian wanted to see in the morning. Her eyes moved to Clara, who smiled at her politely before going back to her nibbling.

"You're like a cute hamster," Adrian teased, patting her head before heading to the frying pan. There were eggs already placed next to it, which the girl cracked one after the other before letting it sizzle on the pan. She watched the yellow yolk spreading as the white outer ring began to form.

"Jimmy," she said, "How's that car coming along?"

"It's on the brink of death as usual."

"In that case, order me a cab. I have to be someplace in the next two hours.

The drive to the office was, as always, a nuisance. When Adrian used the cab for the first time, she was convinced that death was just waiting around for the right moment to take her. The driver was zipping past cars like crazy, almost hitting people and even coming close to crashing the car. When they arrived at the location, Adrian was sitting in the fetal position while the mustached, grinning fool turned around and said, 'your stop, Miss.'

Even that day, the cab was swerving left and right, but Adrian had her head resting on her hand. It's amazing how habits can change so much over time. If anything, she felt the driver was going slow. Seeing that there wasn't the usual traffic, Adrian didn't complain. Better safe than sorry.

The pride meeting was being held at a convention center, a few blocks away from Jimmy's place. Once arriving, she tipped the driver, who sped off an instant later without even thanking her. She turned to see that the doors were closed. Adrian pulled out the flyer to see that it was meant to start at 10 am. It was 9:45 am, so it didn't make sense as to why the place looked empty.

Stepping ahead, Adrian knocked. Nothing happened. He knocked harder, and still nothing. Another attempt, and then she would leave. Right before she was about to touch the glass with her knuckles, the sounds of locks and bolts began. The door opened slightly and someone peeked outside. Adrian could barely tell who it was.

"Yes?" the eye spoke. "Can I help you?"

"Umm, yes. I'm here for the meeting," I said, showing her the flyer.

"Oh yes, yes. Please come from the back door. It's just to the right."

Adrian noticed that the hand the person used to point had missing fingers. An unexpected sight at that early hour. She did as instruct but felt a wave of discomfort. Why the shady behavior? Adrian started to look around for some random fella passing by, who'd later turn out to be an informant for the cops. Walking into the alley, she passed by trash cans and graffiti before finding the oddly rainbow colored square next to a door.

"Ah yes, please come in," said the same voice from before. The door swung open, and the person finally revealed herself.

There was an odd moment as Adrian, a 5-foot 11 heighted woman, stood there, looking at a tiny old woman who couldn't be more than 5 foot 2. She had a bob cut, which kept her white hair trimmed. Her skin as pale as the moon and she carried chestnut brown eyes. Her smile was so endearing that Adrian's heart melted. Had it not been for the hair, she could be mistaken for a child because there were barely any hint of wrinkles on her face.

"Hello there," the tiny lady smiled. "I'm Patricia. And you are?"

"Hi. Adr- Tashia. Is this a bad time?"

"Not at all, my dear. I'm sorry about that back there. We have to be extra careful about onlookers. The last time we kept our location open, plenty of trouble found us. Please come in. I hope you like some hot coco."

Adrian followed her inside. The hallway was dark, which she assumed was deliberate. They entered an elevator in the far distance. Patricia was quick to press the top floor button. The moving machine was dreadfully slow, and they had 20 floors to cross.

"It's always so nice to see new faces joining," she said. "Are you volunteering or here to donate?"

"Well... to be honest, I didn't know about the donation. I do want to help however I can."

"Lovely. We can use all the help we can get. Our march is four weeks from now, and the work is slowly starting to pick up. What do you do, Tashia?"

"I'm... I'm a waitress. And a janitor."

Adrian wasn't entirely lying, but the embarrassment in her voice was enough to make someone doubt. Patricia held her hand.

"There is no shame in the things we do," she assured. "I used to dress up as a clown for children's birthdays back in the day. Believe me, children are all a whole different level of hard work."

Both of them giggled.

"Do you have kids?" Adrian asked.

"No unfortunately," Patricia admitted, sounding disappointed. "I always wanted to adopt but... things just never fell into place."

"I'm sorry. I didn't mean to upset you."

"No worries, child. I have no regrets or anything. Life is a funny thing. Sometimes it gives you the things but at the wrong time. Other times, it never gives what you want but yet surprises you with something. There is no telling what's in store."

"Does that include what's about to happen in the meeting? Because I have no idea what to expect."

"Well then, you're about to find out."

The elevator reached the top floor, and the doors slid to the sides. Both were quick to walk out. For someone so small, Patricia walked fast. Her steps were tiny and quick. There was something comical to it, but Adrian knew better not to giggle. She followed her to find herself facing a room filled with people. Having worked in many places, seeing color was nothing new, but this was a room smothered with shades of so many kinds. People with exotic haircuts, dyed hair, powdered makeup, flashy dresses, and bright faces. Whenever Adrian noticed people looking at her in a particular way, it was a given she would start to feel insecure and unwelcome. There was something different about this crowd. So many of them were smiling at her and observing with kind eyes. Plenty of them stood up to see her.

"Everyone, this is Adrian. She is here to volunteer."

"Hi, Adrian." They all said in unison.

The next thing Adrian knew, was shaking hands, being patted on the back. There were so many compliments being passed to her that it felt like a dream. A short haired black man approached her and shook her hand hard.

"The name's Del," he said. "Can I just say those jeans are mighty fine?"

Adrian felt herself blush, which drew plenty of more attention from the crowd. Tears started to fill her eyes.

"Is everything alright?" Patricia asked.

"It's wonderful," Adrian admitted. "It's probably the first time, in a very long time… where I felt like I belong."

The meeting mostly centered on the issues facing the LGBT community. Prejudice, discrimination, and attacks on their people. The list went on. Certain states in the country had allowed gay marriage, but others felt otherwise. Some of them even provided bathrooms for transgenders people, but incidents would still occur. It seemed that LGBT community found themselves in a bit of a mixed bag. Hope lied in the fact that the younger generation was more open minded and kinder toward their well-being. Yet, there was even a section of youth that resented the gay movement on the basis of morality and religious reasons.

For the first time ever, Adrian felt she was hearing her story, but through the words of those around her. So many of the people in the meeting had experienced horrors. Some were abandoned by their families; others were subject to assault. A few ran away from home, and others never knew who their parents were. It was heartbreaking to see so many people suffer on the basis of their sexuality and biology, and yet it gave Adrian a sense of relief that she wasn't as alone as she had felt all these years.

When everyone had shared their stories, Patricia took the stand and started explaining how the march was to be arranged. They had been given the green light from public office and had managed to take a considerable chunk of the roads in NYC. Four divided groups were to come together in one big bunch. There were still some things left. They march needed security, a lot of marketing, reliable technicians, and people to help guide the movement on the final day. Adrian found herself being placed in both the marketing section, and like most of the crowd, a guide during the final day.

Never before had Adrian just accepted the responsibility that quickly before. Her gut told her entire body that this was what she was meant for. So much awaited her, and she couldn't wait to see what came next.

Once the meeting concluded, Adrian found herself in the company of the openly gay Del and his bi-sexual best friend, Sasha. Both were wonderful company. Del worked as a software engineer in a web house and was gifted in shooting one joke after the other. Sasha was a crew cut, medium height, dark eyed, mix of both Russian and Japanese heritage. Her clothing showcased her sharp, lean arms. The girl was a self-defense instructor and had just opened up her own place. For someone who could be mistaken for being intimidating, she was actually open and friendly.

"You should come by sometimes," she told Adrian, handing her card. "Not only do we keep douchebags in place, but give a fantastic workout as well. However, I don't train hitting computer screens. That's his job."

"If I had a dollar for every time someone wacked their damn screens." Del groaned.

We sat around, eating snacks while most of the crowd started leaving. Plenty had jobs to return to. Patricia joined the three, seeing them all sharing laughs and stories.

"I see you made friends already." She chimed.

"These two are quite a pair," Adrian smiled. "I know technology is tricky, but martial arts also are a mine field of so much movement."

"Trust me, I'd take that over my job any day," Del admitted. "My boyfriend Davis has been insisting for months now. Speaking of which, you seeing anybody, Tashia?"

That question garnered more curiosity.

"No," I confessed. "I've dated men every now and then, but it's generally a short time thing. My... well, my nature doesn't guarantee long-term stuff. Plus, it's hard to meet people in bars and parks."

Del and Sasha looked at one another, and a mischievous smile began to creep on their faces. Both leaned forward as Sasha pulled out her phone.

"You ever heard of Tinder?"

Chapter Four

It's a given that certain things in life are bound to be hard. Adrian was going about passing flyers, attending meetings, and even balancing work. The strip club only needed her for limited hours, and it was evident that Enrique was looking for a replacement. Adrian didn't care. She kept busy cooking for the pride team. A community that was blown away by her culinary skills and gave genuine praise. If something was a bit off with the dish, they'd say so.

Balancing work and being part of a cause sure was hectic, but neither came as confusing and frustrating as online dating. Tinder, unlike anything Adrian had experienced.

Dating was nothing new to her. Since she had been in the big city, it was common that every now and then, someone or another displayed an interest. When she worked as a waitress, plenty of men would try their chance. On some occasions, she'd have her one-night stands, but it never quite went past that. Some were nice enough to give her some money, but it was hard to tell whether they were doing it out of some unspoken obligation or genuine care.

Adrian felt it was best not to ask. She was lonely and had been for a very long time. Any form of intimacy for her went a long way. She knew the relations would be sexual, but it felt nice to be held in someone's arms. It made her feel safe. For just those very moments, Adrian felt what most women took for granted, loved.

With time, it became stale, and Adrian out aside any hint of hope. The cash helped, and she never crossed past with those men again. It also made her realize that she preferred men. What she didn't prefer was when they were being assholes or creeps. Tinder seemed to give plenty of them leverage to be both. For every swipe Adrian did, ten of them would immediately respond. Some were quick to run when they'd find out she was trans. Others took a keen interest just to get an idea. Their stupid questions, however, ensured they lost their chance for further discussion.

Sometimes, without any explanation, guys would just stop talking to her. 'Ghosting' is what they would call it. It was only a matter of time before Adrian stopped responding to matches herself. Feeling little to no luck on the dating apps, she decided it was best to focus her energy elsewhere. Social media was tiring enough on its own.

The pride march occurred with considerable success, but it still faced plenty of obstacles. The public offices had granted permissions, but there were still groups standing on the day, holding up posters on how they were an abomination. Some of the bigots even tried to toss cans over, but they did little to bother anyone. The march was prepared for this. It was a given that they would face resistance, the point was not to fall into that trap. Adrian felt anger surge in her veins when they spat homophobic slurs but decided to shout the protest anthem louder. The feeling was exhilarating. The days of hard work were paying off, and Adrian could see how much a community could make a difference.

It seemed that the march would be limited to one place alone, but a small segment was planning on going to Miami to participate in some of the communities' activities there. Patricia asked Adrian if she was willing to join, and the girl didn't have to think it over much.

"Are you sure?" Patricia asked. "I know you're quite busy here."

"Trust me," Adrian reassured her, "I feel like I am accomplishing with you all, then I feel I ever have cleaning dishes or entertaining perverts."

Patricia smiled ear to ear.

"Then there are many more good things to come."

Since travelling by air was far too expensive, the senior members of the pride community hired a bus. The drive was long, but Adrian loved everything about it. She knew America was a big country, and having been in one of the world's largest cities, she assumed that was mostly what the country was like. She was quite wrong. The more the bus moved on from one highway to another, crossing one town after another, it became obvious that Adrian had misunderstood the vast size of the country. Land stretched on for miles, showing no sign of ending. Every small town they crossed had a culture of its own. This is what fascinated Adrian about the US; with all its diversity, the country had managed to push itself ahead. It still had its fair share of intolerance, prejudice, and corporate greed. It just made the girl a bit glad that the noise of the bustling city was behind her. She saw stars in the sky after ages and inhaled fresh air.

She even met strangers on the way. Most of the small towns didn't take too kindly to their presence, but the bus was quick to move ahead. Some people were surprisingly kind and welcoming. The senior members of the team were given places to stay just to rest and leave the next day. The more of this Adrian witnessed, the more she learned how mixed the world was.

It was easy to fall into the spell of hate, but it was tougher to love. Those who helped the group knew the risks involved. Those who resented their presence fell into the temptation of hurting others, even though they didn't have much understanding about it. Sometimes, the haters could be made to turn to their side with some reasoning and discussion, and sometimes, the supporters turned out to be quite fickle in their support.

Adrian sat on her chair as trees passed by. The sun was shining bright that day and grew even brighter as Miami began to close in. Once they had crossed Jacksonville, the coastline would show up often. This time, it had been present for hours, and before they knew it, in the far distance sat the most awaited words.

"Welcome to Miami."

Beaches, parties, and the shining sun. These three things defined Miami for Adrian. The last time she saw the ocean was back at home. It was so stale and fixated on assisting incoming ships. Here, people were on the sand, having the time of their lives. Never before had Adrian seen such a large crowd like that before.

The party vibe wasn't even limited to the beaches, and it was all over the streets, the shops, and even the homes. They crossed plenty of residential areas where people were laying out and smoking the day away. The casual nature of the place began to seep into the group Adrian was with because Patricia, who was keen to get things done on time, found herself wanting to stroll around more. Adrian and the others giggled when they found her lying in the sand with a joint in hand, along with a stranger.

"You're never too old to have a good time." Patricia justified blushing.

Adrian decided to let loose and went about the place. She mingled with some strangers who took a shine to her cause and let showed her around the sites, from the Bayside marketplace to the Wynwood Walls an even the Vizcaya Museum. Somewhere along the journey of finding new places, Adrian realized that she was sitting on a chair at Coconut Grove. The strangers had parted ways while a few were chatting away close by. Adrian decided to stroll about, wanting to see the pier. Coconut grove was quite a sight with its eclectic mix of restaurants, shops and even business buildings. It was like the hippies merged with the corporate world.

Soon enough, her legs tired, and she decided to dip her feet in the water at the pier.

As much as the experience had been fun, she decided to give the dating app another go. After all, it was a different place, so maybe circumstances could be different. After a few swipes, she matched with a handsome looking man. She had her doubts because she had been catfished once or twice. But who cared? She was going to leave the place in the next few days. Even if the person wasn't what he claimed to be, it'll give her a funny story to look back on.

Some back and forth occurred, and she was taken aback by the man's request.

"Wanna meet?" he texted.

"You barely know me."

"I'd like to. I guarantee I'm better company in person. Not a creep or anything. Just limited on social battery when it comes to typing."

Adrian thought for a moment. She wanted to go with the notion of not trusting a stranger, but she just spent most of the day with many. Maybe one more wouldn't hurt.

"This goes against my instincts, so please prove me wrong," she texted. "But okay."

"I am grateful for your trust. I won't let you down. Where do I find you."

"Come to the pier at Coconut Grove. You'll find me dipping my feet in the water."

"That's weird, I'm pretty close to you. Gimme like ten minutes. You'll see a long-haired fellow struggling to jog."

With that, he went offline. Adrian sat down and did as promise. The water was much colder than she had expected. The first tingle was enjoyable, but Adrian had to keep alternating with her feet, until at one point, the temperature became tolerable. She looked in the far distance where boats moved about and wondered what was happening inside of them. Were people happy inside? Or where they too drunk to care? Was there a lot of them, or were some just occupied with one lonely soul?

The sound of approaching footsteps caught her attention, and there stood probably one of the most handsome men she had laid eyes on for a while. In her entire dating spree, she only managed to be decent looking, but this one was a dashing sight. Long brown hair with curls on the end, thinly bearded, tanned, sharp jawline, hazel green eyes, and broad shouldered. He wasn't ashamed to showcase his hot bod, considering his Hawaii shirt was unbuttoned, revealing his solid chest and six pack. Adrian realized she was staring a bit too long.

"Well, hello there," he smiled, revealing his perfect teeth. "You must be Tashia."

Adrian was at a loss for words. She almost accidentally mentioned her real name before pausing.

"Yes… I'm… I'm Tashia." She stuttered, holding out her hand. "Matthew, right?"

"In the flesh. I knew the app was lying to me."

"What do you mean?"

"You're a lot prettier in person. The display pic doesn't even come close."

Adrian blushed.

"I had a feeling you were a player," she admitted.

"Player is too strong a word. I was hoping more of… a wordsmith."

"Well, that we're still about to find out if that's true."

In all the dates Adrian had been on, Matthew was the first to set precedents that were way too high. They started off playing bowling, then sang at karaoke. Soon after, they had Chinese food, and dessert was around the corner.

"You sure got a strong appetite," Matthew admitted.

"Theres plenty more where that came from." Adrian winked.

The chemistry was flying high between the two. Adrian felt like she had probably known Matthew for most of her life. It was tricky to tell whether they actually had a lot in common in terms of interests or was he just a very talented talker.

There were plenty of girls that passed them by, hoping to get his attention. Some were subtle, and others were blunt. The fact he stayed with Adrian really mattered to her. She had half expected him to leave midway because he came off as someone who wouldn't have a lot of trouble getting attention from others. Yet, Matthew was insistent that they had as much fun as possible on that day. There was a certain warmth and endearment behind his blatant flirtation, and Adrian was loving every bit of it. Yet, as always, there came the part that both had to address.

"Listen, Matthew, we need to talk about something."

"Breaking up with me already? I was just gonna take us swimming."

"I'm serious. We need to address the elephant in the room."

Matthew's smile lessened, and he took a more serious approach.

"Alright," he said, partially concerned.

"I'm not… well… I'm not exactly what you think I am."

"Go on."

Adrian explained. She wasn't entirely a woman before. When arriving in America, she took certain illegal surgeries to balance out certain parts of her body. They were necessary, but they were still scarring. She had struggled for a long time with body dysmorphia and had hardly been in a proper relationship. Matthew had to know what he was getting into.

Adrian noticed she had been talking for much longer than she expected to. She had to simply let him know about her sexuality and body, yet the simple chat turned in to a long ramble. She found herself remembering home, her family when she came to America, and all that happened since. Her eyes noticed Matthew looking at her.

"Wanna run away yet?" Adrian asked.

Matthew nodded from left to right. "To be honest, I kinda had a hint about it," he said. "But… I think I'm more fascinated with your story. Please tell me more."

It was at that moment Adrian realized that this was definitely not going to be another short-lived fling. The handsome man was not just fooling around, and he was invested. Feeling a bit of a flutter in her tummy, the girl continued. The day went on from bright to dark as the sun slowly began to set. Soon enough, the two found themselves together in bed the following night.

Matthew was as blessed in lovemaking as he was in appearance and Adrian was loving every moment of it. They experienced ecstasy, laughter and incredible joy. Rest came easy after, only for them to start again. Once the clock struck 2 am, both were sound asleep in each other's arms. When the sun began to shine through the window, Adrian felt a sense of sadness.

"I have to return to NYC in three days," she whispered. "You know this won't go on for long, right?"

Matthew opened his eyes and sighed but grinned soon after.

"What's your take on long-distance relationships?"

"They don't last. At least from what I've seen in other couples."

Matthew rose up and caressed her cheek affectionately.

"We're not like other couples." He smiled. "We don't do what others do; we make our own path."

"As uplifting and romantic as it sounds, how do we do that? I live miles away. You're here. This what we are enjoying is only possible because we are in each other's presence. The moment I'm back home, this spark will fade."

"Have… have you already made up your mind about this?"

"I don't want to give myself false hope. Matthew, I've been down this road plenty of times, where I have a little surge of happiness, and then it's gone."

This made Matthew walk about the room for a while. He scratched his chin, combed his fingers through his hair, and looked worried.

"Six months." He spoke.

"Six months?"

"That's how much time we invest in making this work. Whether here or elsewhere. Look, I know we just met, but… I genuinely feel that there is something special here."

"Feelings don't last, Matthew."

"Then I'll have to prove you wrong."

The smile on his face surprisingly warmed Adrian's heart. The man was determined. If he was wrong, then at least Adrian would know she was right; she just hoped that regardless of how things go, at least they would end on better terms.

What followed was probably the loveliest yet conflicting relationship Adrian has ever been in. The girl was under the impression that she was the one with strange dynamics, her body being the first thing, along with her broken childhood. Matthew, however, had his baggage as well. To start off, he was married. Not only that, he even had a kid. Like Adrian, his childhood was messed up as well. Raised under a drunk, abusive father and a mother who was sent off to a mental asylum after she tried to set the house on fire. Matthew was not in touch with his one brother, who pretty much left the house early on.

Both shared the sentiment of what it was like growing up in a crappy house, but Matthew didn't have a hard time with other kids. He was social, charming, fun, and viciously flirty. Adrian liked the last quality of his but hated it when he would tease about it with other women. They were quick to fall to his charm, but with time, Adrian started to see that it was just something he did to keep his confidence steady.

Matthew was subject to a thing called ugly duckling. Its when people during puberty are hit hard and find themselves not as attractive as their peers. So, like most, he had to work extra hard to be funny and appealing to others. This helped him garner plenty of flirtation games, but the results wouldn't really come around until he turned 25. He would always smile when recollecting that memory.

"For a decade, I went the extra mile to get attention from girls. Then came 25, and they were driving me around an extra mile just to have my attention."

Having invested a lot in keeping himself in shape, Matthew let himself have all the fun. It was almost as if he was making up for lost time. One of the escapades seemed to have left quite an impression on him, and before he knew it, he was in love. Melissa was the woman who stole his heart and had him change his womanizing ways. They were married after a year of dating. The honeymoon period was passionate, but like most good things, it came to an end, and only then did the couple start to see that they were not quite the right fit. Unfortunately for both, they had a daughter named Annie, and it would be unfair and harsh on her to be a child of divorce. Both partners kept trying, but there was no luck.

Matthew returned to his womanizing to compensate for his lack of intimacy with his wife, and soon enough, trouble got worse at home. He wasn't the ideal husband, but in terms of parenting, Matthew was a loving father. Annie and he would always be laughing and playing together. He would sing her lullabies and make sure he warned her about boys.

"She's just seven." Melissa would point out.

"Well, I wanted to marry my school teacher at eight. So, you never know." He spat back.

Adrian giggled at that story and felt a pang of jealousy for a life that she could never have. Considering that Matthew already had his commitments, it already weakened the chances of those two working things out. Distance was already one thing, and now he had a family on his end.

Despite the obstacles, Adrian had to commend Matthew for his effort. Every two weeks, he would visit her in NYC. Six months in, it lessened to once a month, so Adrian began to visit as well. Her work with volunteering gives her more opportunities to move about. Seeing him smiling ear to ear every time elated her heart, and she would run to him and hug him tight. They couldn't care less about what others around them thought. Love was in the air, and they were willing to do whatever it took. Until… a commitment matter came up.

With the LGBTQ meetings talking a lot about commitment, marriage was a subject that was always hovering around. Patricia was among the women who got married after Obama legalized gay marriage in all states. Unfortunately, her time with her lover only lasted a year; who passed away a year due to illness. There were others who had also experienced loss, but some were still committed to their partners. Adrian noticed there were more breakups and 'situation ships' rampant in her group.

It was a given that, sooner or later, this matter would sink deep into Adrian's mind. Matthew and her had been going steady for about a year, and still, it didn't go past the usual routine of someone visiting and having a romantic getaway. That itself started to lose its charm over time. Adrian wanted something real.

During their walks in the big apple, Adrian brought the topic on the table.

"Matt," she said. "What are we exactly?"

"What do you mean?"

"This. Us. What do you think this is? We've been meeting for over a year, but I can't figure out what we are to each other. I know it sounds a bit kiddish for me to have to ask if I'm your girlfriend, but at least give me something."

"You… want to talk about this now?"

"Better now than never, Matt. Look, I'm very grateful for all that you do, and I've been understanding of your situation at home, but sometimes it feels as if I'm slowly becoming another fuck buddy to you."

"Hey, hey, babe. Don't say that." He insisted, holding my hand. "You mean a lot to me. I've been doing the best I can to meet you now and then. I like spending time with you and enjoy making you happy. You're not some 'get in, get out' situation. As 'kiddish' as it may sound… yes… I'm your boyfriend."

Adrian looked at him for a moment. She appreciated his words, but… it wasn't enough.

"I… I need something a little more than Matt."

He leaned back in his chair and crossed his arms.

"Like what?" he asked, annoyed. "Should I sing it from the top of the building?"

"Matt, don't be like that."

"I honestly don't know how to be right now. It feels as if I say something, it's bound to backfire. Be honest now. What do you want?"

Adrian took a deep breath and exhaled slowly. She felt a few shivers pass through her body before finally admitting it.

"I want us… to get married."

Matthew's eyes began to get wider with each passing second till Adrian could see more of his eyeball than his pupils and iris combined.

"Jesus, Matt! I said marriage, not slavery." Adrian sighed.

"Babe… you know my family would never accept this. I already have my role at home."

"You and your wife are separated. You see your daughter on the weekends. There is no home when you're bunking in with your friends. Why are you still worried about their approval?"

"They are not as kind and understanding as Adrian. The last thing I want is people coming around to judge you."

"You mean to judge you."

A silence followed. Matthew looked genuinely hurt by that comment.

"I'm not ready to make that kind of a comment, Adrian." He admitted, looking away. I can't have my daughter thinking I'm some guy sleeping with another…"

"Woman? Queer? Transgender? Dyke!"

Adrian felt a certain frustration rise, and it began to seethe in her words. All the time spent living in happiness, it seemed that this was probably one of their most honest conversations since their first meeting.

"Your wife goes around sleeping with Steve!" Adrian continued. "Your daughter already has a parent going around town. At least you can be upfront and honest with her."

"She's just a kid, for fuck's sake!"

Adrian took a moment and sipped her drink. Leaning back in her chair, she started to look out of the window. People were passing by just like every day. No matter what happened, life would always move on. Perhaps this was the moment where she accepted the inevitable. She had patient enough with Matt, but either he grew a pair, or she walked.

"I've given a lot to you, Matt," Adrian said, getting up. "But if you're not willing to give me something real, then it's best to end things. We both knew this day would come anyways, so let's not act as if it's our first time breaking up with someone."

With that said Adrian made her way out. Matthew tried to reach out, only to have the waiter stand in front of him and that he pays the bill first. Adrian had already disappeared into the crowd. That was the thing about NYC. There are so many people around that it's easy to get lost in the crowd.

Chapter Five

"Being single sucks!" one of the strippers sobbed.

Adrian did whatever she could to hold back her tears. Mary Lynn had just barged into Jimmy's apartment a few hours back and wouldn't stop venting about her broken heart. Although Clara did her best to soothe her while Adrian rolled her eyes, it became evident that she just wanted the attention rather than a solution.

Jimmy even tried to contribute, only to receive a lash out from the sobbing woman.

"You just don't get it, Jimmy!" she shouted.

"I just said that maybe going for ice cream would help you both." he insisted. "Who doesn't love some-"

"Jimmy, go lift weights for a bit, please." Adrian insisted, patting the crybaby's head.

The big buffed goon made his way upstairs, grumbling to himself. Adrian pulled away to face the hazel eyed white girl who could go on for hours if she wanted. This behavior was a general routine for Mary. She'd meet the 'one' and have a honeymoon period that would come crashing down some weeks later. Sometimes Adrian and the others would make bets about how long it will last or whether she was going to use 'my true lover' or 'my one and only' label. One thing was fro certain whether they were black, white, tall, short, local, or foreign, Mary would be at one of their places, being loud enough to bother the neighbors. That day, Adrian, Jimmy, and inexperienced Clara had their hands full.

The one thing that struck out to Adrian was the fact that the more happy memories the woman kept recalling, the more Adrian found herself coming close to tears. There was always a possibility of Matthew's smile or endearing quality that could bring her to tears. And that is exactly what happened.

The moment Mary mentioned how she met her last conquest at the beach, Adrian broke down crying. This wasn't the classic silent sobbing that others were used to, but like the wailing of a child. Mary herself froze at first before finding herself comforting Adrian. Clara had to switch from one crying woman to the other. The wails were loud enough for Jimmy to hurry down, assuming it was Mary, only to start scratching his head. He made his way to the kitchen, opened his obsolete fridge, and put ice cream in three bowls. Walking back, he placed in front of the three women. No one said a single word. They simply noticed the clatter of the bowls on the wooden table and reached forward.

Adrian munched on hers oddly fast, to the surprise of the others. Clara and Mary stared at one another, confused.

"Something you want to share?" Mary asked.

It was Adrian's turn now. To both Jimmy and Clara's slight amusement, there were two little children crying, and they were the ones being the parents. Adrian opened up about Matthew. Everyone listened and nodded till she finished. What followed was a long silence and an accidental giggle from Clara. All eyes turned to her, who was quick to revert back to looking serious. But then Jimmy even giggled before stopping himself. Adrian noticed a smile on her face, and Mary was already giggling. Within moments, everyone was sharing a laugh and a collective hug.

"I'm sorry about Matthew, Adrian." Mary whimpered.

"I'm sorry about Ryan." Adrian replied.

"It's Bryan."

"My bad."

Another laugh followed.

"We need groceries." Jimmy pointed out. "Who wants to go to the store."

The supermarket was always a nice getaway for Adrian. It was strange how certain individuals at the top had convinced people that shopping would help with their problems. An opportunistic means to profit through people's problems. Classic capitalist. Adrian hated that fact and yet was following it. They were skimming through multiple items, from eggs, bread, paper towels, and even more ice cream.

Clara, in the past few months, was still a quiet soul, but she managed to display more initiative through action. She would point at something, inspect it, nod, and place it into the cart. Sometimes, she'd even have Jimmy place in the cart while he pushed it. It was an endearing sight to Adrian. Mary made her way to the booze section and picked up two bottles of vodka.

"It's only temporary," she promised.

Adrian reached her arm across Mary's shoulder to pick up a bottle of whiskey to add to that. Everything seemed to be going fine for a while till someone hooted in their direction. That behavior wasn't anything new. It's what followed that garnered their attention.

"When did they start letting faggots in here?" the whistler scoffed.

The group turned to find themselves looking at two jacked individuals who were clearly looking for trouble. One of them was wearing a black t-shirt and cargo pants, along with sneakers. His head sported dreadlocks, and his sly grin was blatantly bothersome. The one next to him was a larger fellow, bald, sported a thick french beard, piercing dark eyes, with a tattoo on his neck. Unlike his buffed friend, this one was fairly larger in size and more rounded. Yet the flab on his arms would certainly hurt once he swung.

Jimmy was quick to step up while the women moved behind him.

"You got a problem?" he asked.

"Not with you, pal." the bald one said. "But that queer with you sure got me thinking. Whaddya think, Paul?"

The dreadlocked one snickered.

"Yeah, Tony," he sniggered. "Think we ought to tell em we don't like her kind around here."

"Kind!" Jimmy growled. "I'll teach you some manners."

"It's two of us against you, freak," Tony smirked.

"Think again."

Everyone looked to see Matthew standing there, already prepared for a fight. Adrian couldn't believe her eyes. It was literally something out of a movie.

"Babe," he winked at Adrian. "I'll just get back to you once I'm done with these punks."

What followed would remain in Adrian's memory forever. Jimmy and Matthew clashed with the two punks. It was known that Jimmy was already a hard hitter, but Tony knew how to move around. Jimmy had already swung multiple swings, but Tony was dodging with ease. He clearly was a boxer.

Matthew, on the other hand, managed to move away from Paul's jab and countered with a surprising series of solid punches and a kick. He wasn't lying about the self-defence classes. Adrian just never believed him because he came off as a generic gym, bro. He had the physique but never displayed much movement. Seeing him pummel Paul to the ground, pick him up, and throw him out of the window made it clear he was a force to be reckoned with.

Jimmy managed to land a hard punch to Tony as well, but the punk landed a hard bottle of whiskey on to his head, bringing the poor fellow to the ground. His attention immediately went to Matthew, who already prepared for him.

The fat guy didn't waste any time. He charged head-on, pushing Matthew out the same window. By then, a crowd had already started to form. It was a given that the cops were already on their way. The old mustached man at the counter was already swinging a fist and talking to the men in blue over the phone.

Clara was quick to rush to Jimmy but could barely lift the fallen giant.

"A little help, please!" she pleaded to the others.

Adrian and Mary rushed ahead and felt every inch of their breath leave their body as they lifted a groaning Jimmy to his feet. He tried to take a few steps to gather himself, only to tumble ahead, taking the three women down with him.

"Well, he's out." Mary sighed.

"What about the handsome one outside?" Clara asked.

Their eyes veered ahead to Paul and Matthew. The former pulled out a knife while Matthew still had his fists at the ready. Some passersby jumped at the sight of them and moved away, reaching for his cellphone.

"You got a lot of nerve faggot!" Paul spat.

"You ain't seen nothing yet, prick." Matthew shot back.

Paul lunged forward and swerved his arms multiple times, landing a few cuts on Matthew. Adrian's man stayed on the defensive. Tony was already charging at him, only to be kicked right in his teeth by Matthew's knee. A full right swing sent Tony hard on the cemented ground. Paul didn't relent and continued stabbing, but his stamina finally began to give way.

Matthew seized this opportunity immediately. He abruptly landed a roundhouse kick to Paul's head, which made him almost fly off against the truck next to him. The sheer force of it knocked the punk out of his senses, and the knife fell to the floor. Matthew fell to his knees with exhaustion, and plenty of blood had stained his shirt. He looked to see Tony straggling to his feet. Both looked at one another dead in the eye.

The fat man took one step forward only to be smacked back to the ground with a heavy blow from Adrian. Tony had joined his friend in sleep.

"Holy shit." Matthew nodded impressed before passing out.

It wasn't so often that Adrian would find herself in an ambulance where a man was bleeding to death. The two punks were already placed into the police cars while Jimmy was with both Mary and Clara in another ambulance that was racing alongside theirs.

"Sir, please hold still." one of the paramedics ordered, dabbing the gauze on his chest.

Matthew seethed and crumpled his jaw as the burning sensation passed through his chest. Adrian held his hand tight, crying.

"Seriously, Adrian." Matthew noticed. "I'm the one bleeding here."

"Screw you." she smacked him, much to the chagrin of the paramedic. "I'm worried sick! Why are you even here!"

"Is that your way of saying thank you for helping me out back there?"

"Matthew, we haven't met for so long. How the hell did you even end up in the same place as us? Are you stalking me?"

His expression confirmed her suspicion was right.

"Jesus Matthew!"

"Look… it hasn't been easy for me. But I can't stop thinking about you, and the many weeks have been terrible. If there is anything I've learned, it's that I don't want you gone. I want you in my life."

"Sir." the paramedic said, "Please hold still while I-"

"No! No! Don't!"

The paramedic snipped a chunk of shirt. The pocket tossed out a small square box. Adrian reached for it. For a moment, it felt too good to be true.

"Is… is this…" Adrian wondered.

"Dammit, I had a whole thing planned. Thanks a lot, asshole." Matthew groaned.

"Just doing my job." the paramedic replied, unfazed, applying more gauze.

Adrian opened it to find a diamond ring inside. The stone was so tiny, but it still glinted in the ambulance. All eyes fell on her at that moment.

"Matt…" she gasped, surprised. "I thought-"

"Listen," he said, immediately clasping her hands with his. "I know that there are many obstacles between us. And I know that us being together is only going to get difficult with time in the future. But I want to course through that entire journey with you. Because you make me happy. And I want to be the man that does the same for you. Please take a chance on us."

No one uttered a word. Even the paramedic stopped and stared at Adrian waiting for her answer. Adrian felt the whole world around her shift into something she had never felt before. Her mind was more present in the moment than ever before.

"Say yes." the driver from the front whispered, looking at the rearview.

Adrian smiled ear to ear.

"Yes," she said. "Forever and ever."

The two kissed and embraced.

"I promise I will never let you-"

Matthew immediately went unconscious.

"Oh my God!" Adrian gasped. "What happened."

"It's alright, miss." the paramedic assured her. "I've just given him some anesthesia. He's lost plenty of blood, but he'll make it. Congrats to you both."

The ambulance arrived at the hospital, and luckily, Jimmy was awake with Clara by his side. Adrian was quick to let the others know. They all cheered and came in for a big hug around the unconscious Matthew. Jimmy joined him in a few moments as his head had taken quite a hit. Once Matthew woke up hours later, the two lovers were inseparable. They spent the next couple of weeks making up for lost time. Matthew would return to his wife and hand her the divorce papers before coming back to NYC. A new chapter had begun in Adrian's life. What made her glad was that after a very long time, she felt hopeful again.

That hope, unfortunately, wouldn't last long in the long run. Both she and Matthew knew that there would be troubles ahead. But two years into the honeymoon of marriage, trouble started to brew. It came predictability from Matthew's former family. The couple had managed to get Adrian's documents together, which was definitely a load of the woman's shoulders. She came clean about her name as well, which she had kept hidden from plenty of others.

Yet, Matthew couldn't break the habit pf calling her Trish. They even moved to Orlando to be together, but Matthew was still torn between his responsibilities to Adrian and his daughter. This kept both parties away from one another, but the missus would always compromise. However, as time passed, it became an exhausting endeavor, and frustrations started flying.

Things took a turn for the worse when the bitter ex went ahead and told Matthews's family and hers about what he had done. When her husband went to visit his daughter as per the agreement, he was confronted by plenty of folks from his side and Melissa's. Adrian saw him leave with a smile only to return with a grave expression.

Once the explanation was given, an argument ensued. They had plenty of fights before, but they would always make up. What made this ugly was the fact that Matthew didn't quite display his usual consistency of keeping the union together. Whatever the former in-laws said to him clearly cut deep because Adrian was struggling to get him back on track.

"I can't keep doing this, Trish." He admitted.

"Matthew, we've been together for five years. You can't just call it off."

"I thought we could work this out, but things have changed. I stand to lose my kid over this. Melissa already knows plenty of lawyers. It's only a matter of time before she bleeds my money dry and has our daughter all to herself."

"You can't fall to their bluff. They're just embarrassed. "You're still a good father, a loving husband, and a good man. You can't just give up because of one conversation."

"God dammit Trish! They're gonna take away my daughter from me! I can't let that happen! Regardless of what I do, I know I stand to lose someone or the other."

Adrian knew at that moment who he would choose. She didn't blame him. Any loving parent would die for their child. Now, she just had to accept the fact that she was about to find herself being on her own again. Abandoned by the man she loved for so long. Her hands began to shake, and she was sobbing in an instant.

"Please, Matthew," Adrian pleaded. "I don't want to lose you."

Matthew quickly calmed his temper, walked to her and held her close.

"You won't," he promised. "I'll still be here. We can still make this work even if we're not together."

The absurdity of his statement made it all the worse. Adrian bawled in his arms. The days that followed were more ugly fights till both had drained one another. Neither spoke nor interacted. The silence said more about what was now going to happen.

Matthew left in the following weeks to spend more time with his kid. Adrian hated him for it, but she still refused to let the man be entirely out of her life. She had become accustomed to the fact that people would keep coming and going, but the one thing she could change was perhaps that this one did not have to be gone forever.

The man had done a lot for her. Adrian no longer had to work odd jobs to get by because he helped her find work in better paid positions. He had treated her with love and care and was unlike any man she had encountered. Perhaps destiny simply did not have it said that the two would last forever. Her act of defiance against it was to make sure that Matthew would be around in some way or another.

For the first few months, both separated for some time. Adrian contemplated first staying in Orlando, where Matthew was, but it became apparently obvious that her former lover was too preoccupied with his own things. She didn't have to guess that the man was avoiding her deliberately. She even ended up having a confrontation with Melissa on one occasion that led to both women to a hospital. Since people were biased, they automatically assumed that Adrian was to blame, and she found herself spending the night in jail.

Matthew was kind enough to bail out both his women, but he walked off with Melissa before slipping some money to Adrian. The sight of Melissa smirking at her really boiled her blood. With too many upsetting memories in one place, Adrian paced her things and went back to New York. It was the city that would always pull her back somehow, no matter how far she went.

With another heartbreak in her mind, Adrian began to question a lot about her appearance. Being a transgender woman, she knew the prejudice of people would follow her to the grave. This led her to contemplate whether she was willing to get certain surgeries done to look feminine. It might even go as far as to make her be the woman she was always meant to be.

The moment the thought slipped into her mind; a bit of worry came about. Finance was one reason, but she had people who could help sponsor her. The problem was that those people tended to have mixed opinions on the matter. One of the key discussions that would come up during the LGBTQ movement meetings was getting surgery to alter the body. This was a very dividing matter. Some were ardently against it because they felt it was better to be content with who they were regardless of what they looked like. Others stated that they had a right to fix what was wrong with them. A few were always in the grey. Adrian felt it was best to finally bring up the matter in her next meeting.

Chapter Six

At first, Adrian expected to get a very lukewarm response to considering surgery or hormonal injections to alter her appearance a bit. Much to her disappointment, she received a very divided one. Some people were supporting her immensely, while others thought what she intended on doing was terribly wrong.

Patricia was the only one person that provided her with something of a neutral stance.

"It's not in my place to be telling you what you should and shouldn't be doing," she said. "We may have similar experiences in our sexuality, but we still come from very different backgrounds. This is a decision that you need to make yourself."

Those words provided more calm to Adrian than what the others kept saying.

"You have every right! Follow your own choices. I support you!"

"This is an act against not your sexuality but against us all!"

It was odd as to how everyone seemed so entitled to their belief more out of just being heard rather than providing any legitimate, rational reason. The more Adrian asked around, the more conflicted the matter became. Consulting doctors, on the other hand, was a whole different game. She sensed some undertone of bias from a few, whereas others were keen on helping. The latter clearly just wanted a chance for money and recognition.

This made the advent all the scarier for her. She couldn't even rely on the medical field to help her out of the situation. Being divorced, estranged from her community, and wanting to bring a change in her life that seemed far away, Adrian felt her usual cycle repeating itself again. It was infuriating when things felt familiar, but this time, the woman wasn't going to relent.

Breaking up with Matthew had made the months difficult, and she found a way to use that pain as a drive. Unfortunately, the motivation can only last for so long. Seeing little luck from those around her, Adrian took it upon herself to bring a change in her life in a different manner.

Rather than making the usual grand changes, she decided to change two specific things: her physical and mental health. It was common to see people talk about it, but they made it feel like a trend, which stripped away its authenticity for Adrian. If people were venturing on some personal journey, they clearly wanted recognition from others about it. To accomplish this, Adrian followed three things: going to therapy, joining a gym, and lastly, getting a new job.

Having worked in restaurants for so long and janitorial services, Adrian was done cleaning up other people's mess and constantly had to defend herself. While job hunting, she noticed an open position for a postman in the newspaper. It painted a funny picture in her mind of her in a uniform, knocking on doors, and having to deal with an angry dog. She put it to a side only to come back to it again. Her chances were slim, and there were still some bills she was behind on. Being a postman provided something a little new. A change of setting and a new kind of lifestyle. She was always hidden away or made to look down while cleaning, now, she could move around and place things where they needed to be. There seemed to be more perks than problems. She just prayed that she wouldn't face the same kind of discrimination.

Much to her luck, no one bothered her. The people who took her interview clearly noticed, and they only had one requirement.

"No politics," they said. "We don't let that stuff get in the way of delivering mail."

"You will not find any trouble from me on that matter," Adrian promised.

She was given her uniform and instructions. The first month was spent on training. What was supposed to be a two-week course ended up taking a lot longer because Adrian had a bit of a hard time learning how to drive their truck. Even though she was cleared on the written tests and practical application, Adrian just couldn't get around moving that box metal box with four wheels. It wasn't until the instructor brought Lee on board to train her that made it easier. Lee, although being Chinese, had enough of an understanding of the local Thai lingo to get by. This made communication between the two easier. Both shared plenty of laughs while Adrian made silly little errors.

"Make sure to always look at both rearview mirrors when turning," he instructed. "There is always some moron trying to cut from one side or the other."

"Doesn't insurance cover a situation where we take a bum or two?" Adrian squirmed, trying to turn the wheel. Those things were much heavier than she predicted. Even if she had to make a slight turn, her hands had to rotate a wheel that took so much of her arm's energy.

"It does, but no one really likes those guys paying a visit. Damn salesman always trying to add something a little extra. Management is gonna give you a tough time if those suits come around."

"In that case, you take over."

Both laughed at that as Adrian smoothly made a U-turn. With Lee's help, she was able to finally get her one obstacle out of the way. Soon enough, she was driving the truck while her assigned partners would drop the mail. On other occasions, Adrian had to do that herself. Neither activity was her favorite, but for the first time, she was doing something new. It got mundane with time, but Adrian saw more of the city thorough the window of her truck than anything else before. She would move from the bustling commercial zones to the quieter residential ones, which were her favourite.

Those small houses with lovely gardens and loving families would always melt her heart. It felt partially reminiscent of her childhood area when the kids would get together and play. The warmth in her heart would fade away soon when the ugly memories came along.

Therapy was a lot more emotionally taxing than Adrian expected it to be. She had a lot to unload, and the first few sessions involved simply getting over the awkward moments. She would mess up when the therapist spoke and when she had to. It was comical at first, but with time, both began to communicate with each other better. Ruth was her name, and she had many clients who were transgender before.

Opening up to her was a little scary at first, yet the woman made the atmosphere so comfortable that it felt odd not to let some steam out. Adrian had gone there in the hopes of recovering from her broken heart, but the conversations went back further to the time she was a child and recollected memories she had long forgotten.

It was bitter work to relive what made her so upset. To replay those events that hurt her so badly, but the only way for her to heal was to face her trauma head on. During the sessions, Adrian was surprised to see why she carried a certain perspective. Why did it always feel like there was a repetitive cycle? Why there were so many sleepless nights?

Being given, that perspective opened many doors, and with it came many painful emotions. Adrian was sinking hard into her crying bouts. She slowly realized what was truly driving her decision to alter her physical appearance. After all these years, she was still struggling to love herself fully.

One day she returned to her apartment to hear the phone already ringing. She picked it up and heard some dreadful words.

"It's Matthew. He's dying."

At first, the words went right over Adrian's head. She thought she had misheard. It was Matthew's daughter on the call, which itself was strange because Adrian and her had never met. The only information Adrian knew about her was from Matthew. With his absence for the past many months, she lost touch with whatever was happening on his end. She didn't even tell Matthew about the postal job or the fact that her citizenship was officially legal.

Adrian had always hoped to share the good news of walking in with her green card and celebrate with her man, but the silence between them led her to believe it was best to keep it to herself.

"Say again, dear?" Adrian asked.

"Matthew, my dad… he's dying."

Now, the feeling of dread began to seep in.

"I don't understand, I… how? Where is he?"

"Hospital," the daughter sniffled. "He doesn't have much time. He wanted to let you know. I don't have a lot of time on the phone please note the details."

Adrian did so, feeling the weight on her shoulder grow stronger. It was a lot to take in. Once she had taken the note down, the girl immediately hung up, once her sniffling turned in to sobs.

Adrian had to sit down for this one. Her eyes went straight to the green card, and she recollected a memory of her and Matthew lying in bed together. Matt was teasing her about the picture she chose to put into the card, but Adrian was adamant about keeping it. The teasing sessions turned into a tickling scenario where Adrian burst into giggles and turned red while Matthew kissed her face all over.

The tears began to roll, and within moments, Adrian was sobbing.

Having finished her probation period, Adrian had a decent run for the first two months, but much to her chagrin, the crew around her turned out to be as bigoted as the restaurant crowd. Lee was a fine fellow, but he was transferred elsewhere, leaving Adrian to deal with the monsters. One good thing about delivering the mail was that she didn't have to see much of the team, but they made sure to give her a hard time.

Adrian pushed herself hard to make a place in the postal service, but the more she did, the more negative attention it drew. People were criticizing her for being a sycophant and too eager. The woman was already carrying more mail than required, and she endured the ugly traffic of the city to work done. The latter helped in finding new, faster routes, but they would still come with the strain of being stuck for too long. Driving in LA was like asking for trouble.

With the management already not too keen on Adrian, we weren't that surprised when she requested a leave.

"What for?" her manager asked.

"My... boyfriend is ill. Doctors say he might not make it. I need to be there for him."

"Sorry to hear that." He replied mundanely. "You do understand that this will mess with your record. Taking a leave right after probation isn't ideal."

"Did you not just hear me? My boyfriend is dying."

"You just said the doctor said he 'might' not make it. Sounds like he has a good chance. Plus, I don't have anyone covering the next month's shift."

That was the last straw for Adrian. If this was really going to be their attitude, then they could go screw themselves for all she cared. Sometimes, putting one's foot down is the best way to give a message, regardless of whether the other likes it or not.

"I've told you what the case is. I am taking my leave. If you have a problem with that, find yourselves another driver by next month's time."

With that, Adrian walked out, while the manager pleaded for her to stay. It's amazing how quickly people's tunes change when the unexpected happens. Once she was out the door, she informed Patricia that she won't be attending any further meetings with the group. There appeared to be some passive aggression towards her questioning of getting surgery done.

"I understand," Patricia said. "We all hope Matthew recovers from this."

Adrian packed her things and flew to Matthew. Once the plane landed, she didn't even bother checking into a motel. She went straight to the hospital. The woman was stopped at the door by a confused guard, leading her to throw a tantrum. That was about enough for someone from inside to come and help her out. She was guided to the 7th floor by an intern.

Once Adrian walked into Matthew's room, the sight of him shook her. The once handsome man had thinned down considerably. His skin looked aged, and his hair even began to show some blading patches. He looked at her, surprised.

"Trish?" he wheezed.

Adrian noticed the drip along with the pipe instilled in his neck. The sight of it broke her heart, and she embraced him sobbing.

"Aw babe," he croaked, stroking her hair. "Don't cry. I'm still good looking."

Adrian giggled and cried again.

"Why didn't you tell me, dammit!" Adrian cursed, with her face pressed in his chest.

"I didn't want you to worry. All I've done is give you trouble."

Adrian smacked his face lightly.

"You're an asshole, Matt!" she lectured. "Yes, I know we've haven't been talking for some time, but for God's sake, why would you think I completely wanted you out of my life?"

"You've had so much on your plate. So much pain. I ended up hurting you in the end. I was weak, Trish."

Matthew was fighting back his tears now. His kind face went from concern to complete sadness. Both embraced again, crying like little children. It was almost as if the last few fights between them never happened, and whatever was lost during time was now bridged again.

Adrian spent the whole night beside Matthew. She woke up to see her holding his hand, and a girl standing to her side. She was eyeing her up and down. She was an adorable sight, but was cautious in stature.

"Hello there." Adrian said, waking up Matthew.

"You must be Adrian." She replied, still on the defense.

"My baby," Matthew chimed. The girl was quick to hug her father. "Trish, this is my daughter, Annie."

The girl was close to a replica of her father. Once she would reach puberty, the boys were bound to come running.

"Yes, I am. It's very nice to meet you." Adrian smiled, holding out her hand.

Annie's eyes never left Adrian's. It was blatantly clear that she wasn't happy with her company. The woman assumed it had something to do with her appearance.

"Annie is generally shy around strangers," Matthew assured her. "My dear, why don't you get yourself some yummy Twinkies from the machine."

"Mom said I shouldn't."

Adrian pulled out a five dollar note. The girl's eyes widened, and she beamed.

"It'll be our little secret," Adrian whispered.

Annie hugged before rushing out the door.

"She's a sweetheart," Adrian admitted.

"You can thank me for that."

The two shared a laugh before things got serious.

"How bad is it? And this time, don't leave me in the blank."

Matthew took a deep breath. The woman knew there was no good news coming her way.

"Really bad." he sighed. "Doctors saying that… There is very little chance for this to get better."

"What about chemo?"

"It's a little too late for that. Plus, chemo is not a guarantee. I can't afford that stuff."

"Let me cover it."

"Trish… this isn't a fairy tale. This is the real world. The past few days have been tough because I'm doing what I can to accept what is coming. There is no way to explain this, but my gut tells me this is it. No more second chances, no more extensions."

Adrian stood up and fought back her tears. She moved towards the window, weeping to herself.

"I'm dying, Trish. And I don't want to spend the last of my days simply having people forcing me to do something that'll make me weaker. I've thrown up more times than I can count. I can barely move half the time. Fucking hell, I need the nurse to come and help me piss."

Adrian pondered and knew there was only one way to go about this.

"Matt, I love you," she said. "Since the first day we met, I knew you were the one. Life has its fair share of twists that kept us apart. If… this is really what you want.. then at least let me be with you till your last breath."

Tears rolled down Matthews's weakened face. His cheekbones couldn't be more visible.

"I love you too, Trish." he smiled. "I'm so sorry for fucking everything up."

"Stop talking. Just tell me how we can make this easier."

The next couple had Adrian staying in the hospital. She got closer to Annie but never crossed paths with Matthew's missus. It was upsetting to see that even on his deathbed, she didn't want to meet her husband.

Matthew was like a wounded animal. He needed all the love and care, but he couldn't stop crying over how useless he had become. Adrian heard him out, caressed his hair, and whispered a soothing tune into his ear. Whether he was angry or bawling, it always calmed him down. What made it more difficult was the fact that he would struggle to put up a tough front when Annie would come in, but even the little child could see through his act.

"You're a bad actor, Daddy," she said. "I know you're in pain."

Matthew forced a grin while his daughter helped wipe the sweat from his forehead. With each passing day, Matthew's health took a turn for the worse. Adrian found herself backtracking on her decision but had to stay adamant. Matthew wanted to go out fighting. He was not going to let himself drown.

Two weeks passed, and the doctor made it clear that the end was near. Matthew was not going to get past the next three days. Luckily, that was enough time for him to speak with his daughter. The poor child refused to separate from her father and had to be moved away by the nurses. The look on Matthew's face broke Adrian's heart. She did her best to console the little girl, but all she wanted was to be with her father.

It was decided that Annie would not be present at the last moment because she had already seen enough. Annie was to stay with her mother while Adrian tended to Matthew. The doctors had already pulled the drip from his wrist, and the man slowly began to breathe slower and seemed somewhat calm.

Adrian was the only one present when she woke up to the sound of him giggling about something.

"Matt?" she asked, surprised. "What's wrong?"

"Nothing," he croaked. "Just remembered this stupid joke."

Adrian stared blankly and nodded. The passing moments were getting more dreadful.

"Trish?"

"Yes, Matt."

"Can… can I truly ever be forgiven?"

"Of course, babe."

"No… don't say that because of what I am like right now. Be honest. Have you truly forgiven me?"

"I have."

"Can you help me forgive myself?"

Adrian held his hand and kissed it.

"Matthew, you're a good man. Flawed but good. You didn't have it easy growing up. Despite what life threw at you, you still fought to the last minute. You're an asshole at times, and you're most loving and kind. You are by far, the most perfect man I ever met. It's not in my place to help you do that, Matt. Only you can forgive yourself."

The weakened soul took a deep breath and lost himself in thought before turning back to her.

"I have one request."

"Anything love."

"Can you… forgive those… who wronged you?"

Adrian was confused for a moment.

"Your family. Your friend from school."

"Matt… why would you ask me this?"

"Because you've been so angry your whole life. That anger would come out in different ways, and I would see you punishing yourself in one way or another. All these years, you still carry those bleeding scars in your heart. It's time to stop the hurt and let yourself be free. Trish… promise me."

"I… I…"

"Adrian! You have to promise me that in time, you will come to forgive. Because you deserve to be at peace."

Adrian stuttered for a moment before finally nodding.

"I promise, Matt. I'll forgive them when I'm ready."

Matthew relaxed himself and fell asleep. His hand still had it grip, but once the heartbeat seized, the hand finally let go. Adrian felt a presence that was there for an instant and withered away. There he lay. Matthew. The love of her life, is now in a better place.

Chapter Seven

Adrian had lost plenty of friends over the years in the life of being a stripper. She even knew about a janitor who got shit during a mugging in one of her restaurants. But she had never buried a lover before. Watching his casket being lowered to the ground was by far one of the most difficult things she had to endure. Jimmy patted her back since it was the only thing he could do. Clara's kind words were falling on deaf ears because sympathy for Matt's passing was ringing in her mind by now.

As they walked away, she got one last look at Annie, who was with her mother. Both women looked at one another, and despite it being the time to grieve, Matt's wife looked at her with a begrudging look. It didn't surprise Adrian. In her eyes, she was the other woman. It didn't matter either. Adrian was far too upset to care about her opinion. The love of her life was in his grave and now was the time to contemplate some of his memories.

Adrian, Clara, and Jimmy dropped by a diner where Matt was a regular. The waiter recognized them and simply nodded, pointing to a table. The three took their place and remained silent. Jimmy, as expected, ordered heavy, while Clara and Adrian decided to split some pizza.

Usually the food was always delicious, but Adrian's taste buds were hardly paying attention. Clara had to remind her to continue eating because her food was getting cold. Adrian's attention was stuck on the sight of Matthew's face. The times when he smiled, when he cried secretly, and when he would wink at her as a tease. All those expressions replaced with the face of no life kept pushing the dread in her system.

"Y'know," Jimmy said with a mouthful, "Matt would be happy that we are going to continue this tradition of his."

"I agree," Clara added, "It's such a sweet way of remembering him."

"He…" Adrian choked. "Would… be…"

Clara rushed over next to her and held her tight while Jimmy held her hand. Some people turned and stared.

"Mind your business!" Jimmy growled at them.

The onlookers immediately turned around. Jimmy had a natural gift for scaring others.

"We can leave if you want," Clara suggested.

"No… I just need a moment. I'm gonna use the bathroom for a moment."

No one stopped her. The diner was familiar with Adrian's presence, so no one complained when she made her way to the lavatory. Only one woman complained about her presence. Luckily, others stepped in, and no one has troubled her since.

Adrian sat on the seat for a while, letting her grief out. Usually, she would make an effort to be quiet about it, but it was too difficult to keep it together. She stopped when someone knocked on the door.

"Clara, I'll be another minute." She said, annoyed.

"Hey... you alright?"

Adrian didn't recognize the voice, but it was oddly familiar. She noticed the person on the other side was wearing trainers rather than generic heels or sandals.

"Yeah, yes. I... just need a moment. Nothing serious."

"I know it's strange hearing this from a stranger, but... you wanna talk about it?"

For a moment, it felt too good to be true for Adrian.

"Are you serious?" she asked. "Like I said, strange but not impossible. I can take the seat next to you. We can talk to each other like we're in confession."

"I'm not really one for religion."

"That makes two of us."

Adrian smiled at that. Whoever this was managed to bring a hint of joy. Maybe a small talk wouldn't be so bad. After all, things like these didn't happen often.

"Yeah, okay. Take a… toilet seat."

Both giggled at that. Once she heard the door lock, Adrian took a deep breath. Her eyes noticed the stranger passing a cigarette from the other side.

"No thanks," Adrian said.

"Not a smoker?"

"I am. I just don't want to buzz away my issue."

"I can respect that."

The sound of a lighter flicking echoed in the bathroom.

"Where do you wanna start?" the stranger asked.

"This feels more like therapy than confession."

The stranger laughed at that. It was a cute one, too. Adrian wondered why the feeling of familiarity wasn't going away.

"Well, whenever you're ready to open up."

"My lover passed away three days ago."

The stranger remained silent. Either she went blank and didn't know what to say or just wanted to wait longer before responding.

"Usually, people start offering their condolences when I say that." Adrian sighed.

"Something tells me you've been hearing it so much that it actually might be better to let the moment remain in silence."

"Wow… you got that from my voice?"

"It's a blessing and a curse. Do go on."

Adrian found herself reliving many of the times when she would spend nights with Matthew. How those tender moments were now replaced with the image of his weakening body in the hospital. His once charming smile was now constantly frowning and in pain.

"I know it's a little cliched to say, but" Adrian continued. "He really was one of a kind, like one of those people who had the gift of making you feel special. He could walk into a room, and everyone would just gravitate towards him. It meant the world to me that someone like that would fall in love with me. I know we can't see each other, but I'm not exactly a catch.

At first, I did think he was just messing around. He's playing some game to boost his ego. He proved me wrong. The guy went the extra mile. I guess… because there was so much love coming from his end, it would get scarier when he would be upset about something. I've always been something of a people pleaser, so I never wanted to disappoint him. He helped me get over that, but I could never shake off the fear when he and I would fight about things. Like, would he love me the same after?

He did. Sometimes, I felt he over did it. Since there were so many feelings in the air, I think I can now see why he was so conflicted when it came to choosing."

"Choosing what?"

"Between me and his family."

A silence followed, and I noticed the feet next to me somewhat twitched a little in discomfort.

"Go ahead, say it." Adrian sighed.

"I'm no one to judge," the stranger replied. "I've hurt some people too. Not like I had an affair, but it would be hypocritical of me to point a finger. Please do go on."

"I had a hard time being content with the fact that he chose his family. Selfish to say that, but I honestly missed him. It had been so long since I felt so strongly about someone with such passion.... And now he's gone."

Adrian was surprised to hear a whimper on the other side. The familiarity started to annoy her a bit. Why did it sound like she had heard this before?

"Wow, certainly a first in confession where the priest is crying." Adrian joked to lighten the mood.

"I'm sorry. That really hit quite deep. Clearly not qualified to be a therapist."

"It's cool. If anything, it helps to open up to a stranger."

"Glad to help."

"You want to keep this fair? Like, do you want to share something?"

"Yeah. Your story actually took me back in time."

"How so?" Adrian wondered. Maybe they crossed paths before. It would explain why the person seemed like someone she might know.

"Many years ago, far from this country. I had this friend. Well, we were friends. It… didn't end well."

"Go on."

"I was an asshole. I know most people would say, 'you were young, and you made a mistake,' but the age factor is hard to justify when you already know the difference between right and wrong."

"What happened to this friend?"

"I hurt her. I… My father served in the army, and he got transferred overseas. Since the distance was so far, he didn't want the family to be apart, so he brought us all along. I joined this school and made a friend. She… she was a sweet soul. She was kind and considerate, but the poor thing was subject to a lot of hurt."

Adrian's heartbeat began to pick up pace. It couldn't be… could it?

"We became close, but looking back, I guess I'd given the wrong message. She started to… like me. As in more than a friend. This made things awkward, and I decided to distance her. It was the last set of days when our class got together for an outing near the lake-!

"Jane!" Adrian gasped.

"Wait... how did you-"

The stranger jumped the moment her door flung open. Adrian stood there looking at her with utter shock. Her once former friend from school sat there, right in front of her eyes.

The girl of her dreams from once upon a time had grown up to be quite an attractive woman. The only thing different about her was the spectacles she had on.

"You!" Adrian seethed. "How... when... what the fuck are you doing here!"

Jane's expression changes from shock to guilt.

"Adrian.... I... didn't even..."

The woman was at a loss for words. Adrian felt an anger surging through her that led her open hands to tighten into a fist. She smacked it against the door, which garnered plenty of attention.

"Excuse me," another came walking. "Is there a problem?"

"Mind your business!" Adrian snapped before looking back at Jane. "I don't know what kind of sick joke the universe is trying to play here, but I sure as hell am not falling for your shit! All these damn years later, and you can still make me feel so damn angry and bitter!"

"Please, Adrian. Let me explain. I didn't even know it was you until-"

Adrian was already making her way out of the bathroom. She went straight to Jimmy and Clara, who didn't have to guess that trouble was brewing.

"You want me to parcel?" Jimmy asked with a mouthful.

"No. We're going."

"We ought to pay the bill at least." Clara insisted.

Adrian dropped a twenty-dollar note and was on her way out while the other two clumsily tried to catch up. Jimmy's abrupt movement caused the tray of dishes to shatter to pieces on the ground.

"Sorry. My bad. What about the change? Are we tipping heavy?" he called out.

Adrian probably whistled the loudest at that moment, that two cabs stopped dead tracks in their tracks. In all her years in NYC, that was the first time it ever happened. She immediately jumped in while Jimmy and Clara stumbled multiple times before getting into the door. Right from behind them, the spectacled, blonde beauty came rushing.

"Get in, dammit!" Adrian shouted.

Clara dived in while Jimmy struggled to fit himself through the door. Jane finally managed to catch up and leaped towards Adrian's window.

"Adrian, please!" she pleaded. "Let me talk. You've no idea how long I've been looking for you!"

Adrian was having none of it. She rolled the window up and gave the driver a piece of her mind to hurry.

"You're not getting tipped at this rate!" she threatened.

Both Jimmy and Clara had seen her angry, but this was a whole different person. The cab had already started moving, while the former's leg was barely in the door.

The driver pushed his engine and swerved around a few close calls. Jane struggled to catch up and had to stop at one point. She watched as her one chance of redemption moved further away.

Adrian took one look at the rearview mirror and held out her middle finger to the girl that broke her heart all those years ago.

"The fact I even opened up about Matthew to that bitch!" she spat.

Jimmy and Clarice looked at her awkwardly but didn't say anything. Something had come over their friend, and they were now going to be curious for answers later. Adrian was about to reach for something until she realized her mistake.

"Fuck… I forgot my purse." She groaned.

"You want me to turn around?" the driver asked.

He regretted it the moment Adrian stared at him.

"Right, straight ahead. Of course." He smiled weakly.

With each passing day, Adrian found herself muttering curse words and hitting things harder than needed. Jimmy and Clara would jump to the sound of banging doors or the clamping of a hammer on the wall as their friend tried to hang up a photo. Jimmy was too scared to request for the hammer and endured the never-ending thumping in the house. They were louder than his barbells hitting the ground.

Clara was patient with this behavior for only the first three days. The constant cold shoulder started getting on her nerves. As much as she had become familiar with how the house worked, there were always moments when she needed a helping hand. Adrian's frequent passive aggressive mood was not helping. The girl tried her luck in getting most of the usual things done on her own but then came the dinging clock.

Jimmy had a habit of collecting old relics and was in awe with an old school clock that would make everyone's ears ring when it struck twelve. One day, the clock struck noon and wouldn't stop. Jimmy tried his luck the best way he knew how, smacking it with his large palms. Each strike made him guilty, and he would pat it kindly before smacking it again.

Clara kept trying her luck by trying to understand its structure, but the clock really was a product of its time. There was no off button or lever to turn the damn thing off. Clara's head was throbbing when Adrian burst through the door.

"Turn that damn thing off!" she blared. Whatever she said next was overtaken by the clock's ringing.

"I'm doing all I can," Clara replied, annoyed. "This damn thing just wouldn't-"

The girl lost her balance and fell to the floor hard. Jimmy rushed ahead to pick her up while Adrian fumed and tossed her shoe at the clock with full force. It hit the dead center of the clock which made the noise stop in an instant.

"Hey!" Jimmy announced. "That almost broke it."

"It's already broken, stupid!"

That made Jimmy become quiet immediately. Despite his toughened physique, the man was always insecure about his lack of intelligence. Right at that very moment, Adrian had managed to cut right through him and she knew a line was crossed.

"Take that back," Clara demanded.

"Screw this," Adrian scoffed. "I'm heading out anyways."

"Hey! You owe Jimmy an apology."

"I don't owe shit! This place runs because of me."

Clara stared, dumbstruck. It became clear that it wasn't her friend she was talking to.

"What the hell is the matter with you?" Clara asked, crossing her arms. "You've been a dick about everything since the diner."

"As a grown adult, I'm entitled to some privacy and understanding. I just lost my husband! Things aren't exactly all bright and sunny!"

"Trish, we all feel for your loss. Yes, losing a loved one is hard. I would know, having buried a baby brother. But don't for a second think that justifies you being an asshole! We've been tiptoeing around for a while now. And I don't believe this is entirely about Matthew."

"Clara, you're walking on some very, very thin ice."

The girl sighed and gestured at Jimmy to leave. The giant sulked on his way out, giving one stinge of guilt in Adrian. The moment the door closed; Clara let out a deep sigh before looking straight at Adrian.

"Okay," she began, rubbing her eyes. "Who was she?"

"Who?"

"For the love of God- Adrian, she followed our damn cab for a while. Clearly, there is some history there."

"And that's none of your business!"

Clara could see that this was one discussion that wasn't going to happen. Maybe later, when both were calm, but for now, she had to play ball.

"Take a walk, Trish," Clara said. "A long one. While you're at it, at least be honest with yourself."

"Already on my way out."

Adrian stormed out the door and was walking about in the NYC streets. The sight of Jane had triggered something in her, and all she could do was feel bitter about everything. The fact her purse got left behind was another source of frustration, but the woman wasn't ready to have her past just jump out of nowhere. The situation made her long for Matthew because he understood how to go about this, but being reminded of his passing just made it worse.

Since she had already screwed things ups at home, she decided to call upon the one person who could help. He was already visiting the big city, and Adrian didn't want to keep him waiting, Magnus.

Chapter Eight

Settling in the biggest city in the world had its fair share of troubles, and Adrian had been lucky with plenty of people during the early days. One of the few people who made a good impression on her was Magnus, a Danish fellow who ran an orphanage in Cambodia. Since he was always travelling, the two couldn't meet as much, but whenever they did, it was like they were in touch for the entire time.

Magnus was a funny one, but Adrian never admitted that it wasn't much of his jokes that she giggled at but his accent. With time, it got easier, but she knew she'd be smiling when meeting him again. Despite her friendship with others, Magnus was a special one. It was he who helped her out with her ISBR.

All of the basic stuff was mostly handled by him. He was the only one who insisted that she leave her stripping life behind and pursue something more meaningful.

"It's easy for you to say," Adrian chirped. "You don't look like me here."

"Fair point," he replied. "But I look like this in Cambodia. People want to kidnap more often than I'd like to admit."

Both would share a laugh to that. Magnus was one of the few people who never made her feel uncomfortable and knew plenty of the dark times the woman had endured. He even gave Adrian and Matthew a moving speech during their wedding over a video call. All the kids behind him joined in on a song.

Seeing that an old face had returned to her life, Adrina felt the strong urge to vent about Jane to her friend. She arrived at his apartment, which had a wonderful view of the city. Unfortunately, privacy was not a thing because there was always some stranger on his or her balcony having a drink or a couple getting touchy with one another. Adrian knocked on the door and saw a newly bearded Magnus smiling at her.

"Oh my God!" Adrian gasped, hugging him tight. "You found religion after all."

"It's strange how two weeks of laziness can make others wonder you're a monk! He chimed. "So good to see you, Trish. Come on in. I just finished making some homemade burgers."

"Wow, the most American meal ever. Are you that glad to be home?"

"Yes and no. It's always nice to be back in New York. But I can never stop thinking about things back in Cambodia."

"You care too much for kids. Why aren't you married?"

"I guess I'm better at being a surrogate parent than an ideal husband."

"In case you change your mind, I'm sure I can play Cupid for you while you're here. That beard needs trimming, though."

Magnus went quiet for a bit, placing the food on the table and taking his chair. Both had a sip of their beers and observed the view in silence.

"How are you, Trish?" Magnus asked.

Adrian knew from the depth of his voice that this wasn't the usual kind of question but a much deeper insight that he needed.

"It's been... rough. Since Matthew left us."

"I can't imagine. He was a good guy. Easily conflicted, but he had his heart in the right place."

"I just wish he had been more vocal about it."

"He was a chatterbox in my memory."

"You're too polite and more of a listener. He always looked forward to hearing your stories in Cambodia."

Adrian munched through her burger, and as always, Magnus's cooking skills didn't disappoint.

"Please, for my sake, become a chef, man!" Adrian moaned, letting the taste relish in her mouth. "I know countless places that would love to have you in their kitchen."

"The only kitchen I enjoy is the one that feeds the kids. Customers in a restaurant always behave as if they're entitled. A child will cherish what is being given to them."

"Your meal is making me behave just like them right now."

Magnus gave a look that was hard to decipher. Adrian managed to finish the remaining chunk and gulped down the beer in a few swigs.

"Wow, sure got me one helluva appetite prepared for this," Adrian admitted. "You got more?"

"Sure," Magnus said awkwardly, "Why don't you munch on those fries while I get some more."

"Refill on the beer, too, please."

Magnus paused midway through the door before moving ahead. He returned with a tray of mini sized burgers and a bucket of beer, placed in ice.

"Oh my God!" Adrian gasped. "Are you in love with me already?"

"Dig in, Captain."

Magnus watched as Adrian devoured one burger after the other. It made him happy that his friend was enjoying his work, but he knew that her behavior meant something was up. Somewhere in the middle of finishing her second bottle, Adrian noticed that Magnus seemed to be waiting for something.

"What's the matter?" Adrian asked.

"I should be asking you that right now?"

"Whaddya mean?"

"I know you got something bothering you when you hog through the food really fast."

Adrian put down the bottle and the food in her hand.

"Open up, Trish, cuz I get the feeling this isn't entirely about Matthew."

"You... you remember my time back in Thailand."

"Yeah, you were bullied a lot in school, and home was a whole different ballgame."

"Yeah, and there was this girl."

Magnus wondered for a moment before his eyes went wide.

"You're not serious?" he gawked.

"Yeah, after all these years. Jane popped up out of nowhere."

"That's... wow... that really is some blast from the past stuff right there. How did it... never mind. Stupid question."

"Ask away, Magnus. I am more confused by it all. And honestly... I'm not handling it well. Jimmy and Clara have had to put up with more. I... really screwed up there."

"Did you say something to them?"

"I called Jimmy stupid."

Adrian pressed her face into her palms. A bit of whimpering began to emerge. Magnus was quick to walk over and let her rest her head on his shoulder.

"Dick moves there, Trish."

"I didn't mean it. The big giant just got upset about his clock. I... the anger that was supposed to be thrown at Jane ended up at him and Clara. I sure love to self-sabotage. The two people that are trying to help me are the ones I'm lashing out at. Whereas the asshole that screwed me over is nowhere to be found."

"You want to find her?"

"No. No, that's not what I meant. I hope she stays away. I..."

"Trish, getting some contradictions here already. Take a breath. Let's think this over."

Adrian leaned back in her chair and put the food down. She stared at the view before noticing a fat guy on his balcony scratching his fat tummy. She looked away in another direction and reminisced about the past. It had been so long that she found herself recalling some memories that she had long forgotten. It was like watching a very moving movie with an unhappy ending.

"She meant a lot to me," Adrian admitted. "I had no one back home. Jane changed all that. For the first time, I had a friend. Dammit, since I was a small kid, I didn't have one. Kids are some seriously mean people. They could tell something wasn't quite right about me. My parents were called in, and I was reprimanded repeatedly to behave a particular way. Imagine years, so many damn years of your life growing up and feeling alone. Then, one day, this beautiful girl comes out of nowhere and makes you feel special. Matthew wasn't the first person to make me feel like I was important. That I mattered.

It felt unreal, Magnus. I would pinch myself many times just to check that I wasn't dreaming. I would even ask her why she wanted to be friends with me. There were plenty of other kids that would love to have her around. She wouldn't hear any of it. It was always about making the most of our youth. I was happy, Magnus. I was so happy to find someone who was good to me. I guess... I just didn't know how to go about it. There were so many emotions running through my naïve mind."

Magnus raised an eyebrow. He was vaguely familiar with Adrian's story but knew that certain parts were left out. At best he was just aware that a girl named Jane came into her life and hurt her. How, when, and why remained a mystery. He would avoid asking a lot about it since it was a touchy subject for his friend. But now felt like the time to finally open that door.

"Trish, heart to heart this time," he said, picking up his beer. "I don't press on this cuz I know it upsets you, but now it appears you holding things inside is just making it worse. As your friend, I'd like to know… what exactly did Jane do to hurt you?"

"She… made a mockery out of me in front of the other kids. There was this badly put together poster that they made of me and my body. Joining like different body parts to show how unnatural it was. It happened at this stupid bonfire. Everyone wanted to celebrate one last time before we went our separate ways. I'm sure they had fun. While I shittiest day of my life. It was so humiliating that I just ran home, gathered my things, and left. I've never looked back since."

Magnus listened closely, trying to piece the puzzle together. There was one matter that kept nagging at him.

"Trish, why do you think Jane did that to you?" he asked, sipping his drink.

Adrian looked at her friends' eyes. Much to Mangus's surprise, there was some hint of confusion lingering there. Either that or some sense of denial.

"I… since Jane was so sweet to me, I… started to like her."

Magnus raised an eyebrow.

"Oh, c'mon man!" Adrian said, annoyed. "I had a crush on her! You follow?"

"If it were a crush, you wouldn't be overwhelmed as you are currently," Magnus pointed out. "You were flat out in love with that girl."

Adrian looked away, crossing her arms.

"Trish," Magnus continued. "There is no shame in admitting that. Anyone in your position would have developed the same feelings. I would go head over heels for a girl who'd give me that kind of attention. I wonder though… is that the reason why she decided to screw you over in front of the others?"

"I… am honestly not sure. I mean, I kissed her, but"

"Wait, what? Did she know that you felt that way about her before doing so?"

"Are you seriously telling me that it was my fault?"

"No, Trish. I'm realizing that before you even told the girl you liked her, you went straight in for a make out session."

"I was a kid, Magnus! Forgive me for not knowing how to handle kissing etiquette!"

"Do you feel that kissing her is what got her upset?"

Adrian pondered over that for a moment, but only a moment.

"I say it's possible." She admitted. "I mean, I get it, I lived in a place where that kind of stuff was frowned upon. I mean, here I am in the land of the free, and still get slurs thrown at me. I just never quite understood, why go that far?"

"You're not gonna like what I say next, but... maybe now is your chance."

Adrian's gawked at that suggestion. She took another swig of the beer to fathom what she just heard.

"You're not serious!" she gasped.

"Trish, hear me out. A lot of this feels almost like the universe giving you a chance that people would spend their lives hoping to find. You had a person change your life in both ways, and that led to a situation where you left home. Now, years have passed, and that question mark has been hanging around ever since. In a city of millions, that one very person comes back into your life. I mean... that's like winning the lottery of life. You have a chance of not just finding out what happened and why. Maybe there could be a piece of the story that was missing. Or I'm wrong, the girl was a bitch all along, but at least you would finally know."

Adrian remained silent. It was a lot to take in. And she'd be lying if she said the thought of finding out the truth hadn't crossed her mind.

"Magnus, what if I'm not ready?" she asked. "Even after all these years, despite everything I have accomplished… I still don't have the guts to face my past."

"Why are you still scared, Adrian?" Magnus asked, sitting next to her and letting her rest her head on his shoulder. "What is it that frightens you?"

"That I might not be able to handle what the truth actually was. Regardless of what it will turn out to be."

Magnus put his arm around her as she fought back tears.

"I have faith in you, Trish," Magnus assured her. "Even Matthew believed in you when you were unsure. You've come a long way from the moment you landed here on a boat. Despite all the crap thrown your way, you've made a life for yourself. You have friends you care about. You're now working towards helping others. You're by far one of the most matures and kindest people I know. If that's not growth, I don't know what is. Before you decide on anything, let's finish the meal."

And so, they did, and once the last bite was taken, Magnus waited for the answer.

"I'll... I'll see what I can do." Adrian said. "But first things first, gonna have to apologize to Jimmy."

Magnus gives her a smile and an approving nod. Both of them made their way to the door as Adrian felt it was time to leave.

"You sure you don't want me there with you?" he asked, just in case.

"No. I appreciate it, but this was my screw up. I'll make it right. Thank you, Magnus. As always, you've been more of a blessing than a friend."

"Part of my Danish charm, I guess. C'mon. Give me a hug before you go."

Adrian pulled him in a tight one and even picked him up, much to his laughter.

"I really ought to start lifting weights if this is supposed to ever get even." he smiled.

"Good luck with that. Your tummy is showing already."

"Last chance for assistance."

"I can handle Jimmy, Magnus."

"I meant about Jane. That's a much deeper matter."

"Let me think it over. I get your point, and yes, plenty of what you said did get across. But I want to make the decision when I feel ready. Rushing it just feels like I'm trying to sweep it under the rug."

"Fair enough. You get home safe now."

Adrian walked on the streets feeling a sense of relief. Magnus had a natural gift for giving another perspective on a matter, which made things a little easier to handle. Adrian had insisted that he pursue becoming a therapist, but he always said he had too much on his plate. Running an orphanage had its fair share of troubles. What impressed Adrian about Magnus was that he could always settle down in NYC and start something for himself there, but he chose to go to Cambodia because his attachment to the kids had become so strong. He would never be able to live with himself if he abandoned any of them. Even these short breaks he would take would have him eager to return.

Adrian didn't want to make the big guy sob for too long. The guilt was starting to hang heavy on the top of her head. On her way to Magnus, she was fuming more, but now that angry storm had reverted to a sullen sky. She and Jimmy had their spats plenty of times before, but the deal with the bouncer was that he always felt insecure about his intelligence.

The guy was laughed at by other kids because he struggled to read and write. When puberty came along, the kid was now bigger than most of his peers and naturally tougher. Soon, he found himself getting into fights. It was only a matter of time before pimps and opportunists would approach him and promise him some dough for a little protection. Once they sensed that he wasn't too bright, they'd try to take advantage of him. Some got lucky in getting away, but others were not. There was a reason why no one messed with that tough titan.

Adrian had just broken the tough fella and didn't feel good about it. Luckily, she knew what would cheer him up. Ice cream sandwiches. A lot of them. Since the first time Adrian met Jimmy, he would always be smiling at the sight of those. She headed over to the closest grocery shop and bought plenty of sandwiches. Before she knew it, she walked out with some food for Clara as well.

It took a moment for Adrian to recollect that Clara had come a long way since the first time she was at Jimmy's place. From the frightened girl to standing up when things got out of hand. Both Adrian and Jimmy were supportive of her and had to be patient for her to open up. She was surprisingly quite comfortable around Matthew as well, which was the man's superpower over others.

Adrian noticed Jimmy's place in the distance and picked up her pace. Much to her surprise, Jimmy was already outside, sitting on the clumsily new made steps. His head hung low and he was plucking the grass in the corner. The sight of him was enough for Adrian to feel bad.

"Hey, big guy," she said, standing in front of him. "I got you a little something."

Jimmy looked up and reached for the ice cream but didn't show that much enthusiasm.

"These are your favourite, Jimmy."

The giant was quiet and finished the first sandwich in one bite. He held out his hand for another, so Adrian handed him the bag. Clara popped out the door. Noticing Adrian, she crossed her arms and leaned against the door.

"Listen," Adrian began. "What I said and did was wrong. It wasn't fair of me to react this way. And I don't mean just for now, but the past couple of days. A lot has happened recently and I guess I am not handling that well. Losing Matthew has been very painful. He was a special soul and now with his death, I strangely feel alone again. I suppose I felt a bit scared too. But I see now that I still have you guys. I don't want to hurt either of you. I just lost my temper because of…"

"That blondie you met at the diner?" Clara finished.

"Yeah. That blondie at the diner."

Jimmy turned to look at Clara, who also looked back at him. Jimmy patted the step next to him for Adrian to sit. She did just that, and Clara sat next to her as well.

"I know," Jimmy spoke with an odd tone of maturity. "I know that Matthew's passing was going to be difficult for all of us. He was nice to me, too. I never felt like I was being made fun of. He took an interest in my workouts and what I ate. He, in fact, helped me fix up my gym equipment. Found work for me where I could use my big muscles. I, too, am very sad, knowing he isn't coming back. I knew that you will be hurt the most. I just… wasn't ready to face how upset you'd become. And I am not sure if this anger is entirely about the girl at the diner or Matthew's death."

"I second that," Clara added. "There are two pieces in this puzzle, but you're not helping us in putting them together."

Adrian thought for a moment while handing out snacks to each of them. It was a little comical how they simply took it but kept their faces stern.

"It's both, to be honest," Adrian admitted. "It's so many things coming at me all at once. I just got overwhelmed. And how I am choosing to go with that… is downright stupid."

Clara and Jimmy eyed one another again while continuing their snack. Adrian wiped a tear before continuing.

"I am sorry, Jimmy," she said. "I hurt your feelings. You're not stupid. I am just an asshole. And I'm sorry to you too Clara. You're not some inconvenience here. If anything, you're one of the most genuine souls I've come across. You are valued here, and I mean that."

Clara leaned her head on Adrian's shoulder while Jimmy pulled them both in for a hug with his one arm. Tears rolled, laughter was shared, and all was forgiven.

"I do have one question," Jimmy said. "What was the deal with that woman at the diner?"

"Let me tell you guys a story."

Chapter Nine

The cold months had finally come around, and people walked into the big city wearing jackets and scarves. Adrian never minded the cold and liked to dress up a little suave when moving about. She had just finished a therapy session and came out more relieved that day. Patricia was a helping hand in that matter. Adrian didn't attend many of the meetings with the LGBTQ movement, seeing as to how conflicted they were regarding her decision of getting surgeries and hormonal therapy.

The passive aggression, along with the undying support from others, made the group something of a minefield. Adrian never liked having to walk around eggshells, and now the group seemed to have caught on that. Patricia remained genuine out of the lot and encouraged Adrian that before coming to a decision, it was best to first really dive deep into the matter. Both internally and externally.

With a good session behind her, Adrian was making her way back home, where Jimmy and Clara had a birthday cake ready for her. Adrian accidentally came across the cake because Jimmy forgot to hide it in the new refrigerator they had just gotten together. The thought made Adrian giggle. She received a text, instructing her that a pipe was leaking and they had to go to Matthew's favorite diner. The trio had gone there right after she had told them about Jane. In order to let her conquer her fear, Clara took Adrian's hand and made sure they visited the same place.

"That place was ours," she said. "We're not letting the past get the better of that."

Much to Adrian's relief, Jane was not around. No matter how many times they went to the diner over the following months, Jane was nowhere to be seen. It made the whole experience a lot more comfortable.

Adrian knew there wasn't a leaking pipe. It was just a ruse to have her head to the diner where the two would bring up the cake. The woman hoped she could put on a convincing front of being surprised. She took a long look at herself in front of a mirror inside a shop. While combing back her hair, she decided to pick up a bottle of water. The session that day had her talking more than usual.

Since an old face had caused such a reaction, Adrian wanted to dive deeper into how much she was still hurting internally. Her therapist, Melinda, and she started off a bit awkward, but with each passing session, it got easier for Adrian to open up. Now they were at a point where the silences didn't bother her. She could sit, contemplate, and start again.

That very day, since her birthday was the subject of discussion, she mentioned how hers wasn't celebrated as much. She barely had any memories of the others because the house wasn't quite affectionate in nature.

When Adrian reached NYC, she had celebrated her birthday only a few times. The first time she had one was at a park among strangers. She was surrounded by a couple of college kids who were listing important dates on a chalkboard. When Adrian passed by, they asked for her date of birth. It just so happened that it was on the same day. Since Adrian had crossed an entire ocean, she was still one day ahead, thinking her birthday had passed the day before. It was an odd moment for her when the young strangers circled around her and sang her a song. Out of kindness, some of them even bought her some cake. It was among the earliest and kindest memories she would go back to.

From then on, birthdays became a yearly thing, but it was common for her to celebrate late or miss it altogether. With time, she made it a personal matter of celebrating entirely on her own. It wasn't until Matthew came around that birthday became such a big deal. Adrian enjoyed not just the amount of attention, but also how Matthew would give it to her. Singing songs, making her dance, and even playing games that were generally meant for kids. It was for her to catch up on a childhood that was missed.

Adrian admitted to Melinda, that now it seemed to be becoming a way for her to reminisce about Matthew rather than focus that she was getting a year older. For that day, Melinda guided her on being more present in the moment. It was easy to let thoughts get the better of her, so for the time she was spending with Clara and Jimmy, her mind had to be there. Enjoying every moment.

Adrian's thoughts immediately ceased when she felt her heel break. She accidentally stepped on a bad crack on the pavement, and now her footwear paid the price. Since the duo would already be on their way to the diner, Adrian felt it was best to rush home, put on a pair of comfortable sandals and then head to the party. The house was closing in on sight when a familiar figure appeared at the cemented stairs. Adrian wasn't sure as to who would drop in to visit them at the evening hour. The person was wearing winter clothes and a hat. Adrian hoped it wasn't some guy hoping to break in.

"Excuse me," Adrian said to the stranger. "Can I help you?"

The person turned, revealing herself to be Jane. Adrian choked and stepped backward.

"You again?" she gasped.

"Adrian. Thank God, I found you."

"How... where... why!"

"You left your purse and wallet at the diner. I had been pondering over whether to come here and visit you in person, but..."

Her voice trailed off. The cold breeze in the air now felt chilling to the bone. Both the women looked at one another's eyes.

"Please, Adrian," Jane insisted. "I just want to talk. You have no idea how long I've wanted this."

The wronged woman noticed how odd it felt for Jane to call her by her former name. She was so used to Trish, and now a familiar from years back referred to her as Adrian. With the name, she was bringing back so many things. Luckily, Adrian took a few deep breaths that she had practiced with Melinda and calmed her mind. She didn't want another outburst like before.

"Wait here," she instructed. "I need to get something from inside."

"Want me to help?"

"No." Jane heard before the door slammed in front of her.

Adrian quickly rushed to the bathroom and splashed her face with water. It occurred a little late to her that she had undone all the makeup from some hours back, but it didn't matter. Making a few changes to her appearance, she took a few more breaths. Somewhere in between her decision to change her shoes and drinking water, Adrian began to do it all slowly. Jane could wait. She needed to be calm if this conversation was indeed going to happen. Adrian recollected her therapist's advice on facing an unexpected situation that is overwhelming.

"Breathe slowly. Take your time. Remember to stay in the moment. Don't let your thoughts overwhelm you. It's you who is in control, not the other way around."

Having taken the last sip of water, Adrian made her way out to Jane, who was leaning against a pole. Noticing her, she straightened up.

"You changed your look." she pointed out.

"Follow me," Adrian replied.

"Where are we headed?"

"The park."

Winter wasn't necessarily that welcoming to people in NYC, yet it never stopped people from coming for a run.

Young couples would be running together, while some granny would be watching over their grandchild. Adrian and Jane were the odd ones that day, being two women who were strolling in complete silence. Any passer-by could assume they were probably arguing some moments ago.

Adrian pointed to a ring-shaped bench, and both sat down. Jane positioned herself to be more prim proper, while Adrian sat more relaxed.

"Quite chilly, eh?" Jane tried. The look on Adrian's face made it clear there wouldn't be any more small talk.

"Get to it, Jane," Adrian said.

"Adrian, I... the fact I never knew this day would come. I always imagined what it would be like, and now that it's happening, I couldn't be more unprepared. Despite that, know that whatever I say is the truth and nothing else."

"You do know that I have plenty of reason to doubt that."

"You do. And it's justified. But please give me the chance of a listening ear."

Adrian sighed and crossed her arms.

"Make it count, then."

"Alright. Many years ago, I did something very cruel to you. I abandoned you at a time when you needed love and care. I left you. That has haunted me for so many years. I was confused, Adrian. I was taken aback by the fact you made a pass at me. Let alone had feelings for me. Instead of being sensible about it or giving you the chance to say something, I let you go. I thought with time, perhaps I would be able to come to terms with it, but it's always bothered me. There were days when I couldn't even sleep. Getting to see you finally brought so much of those feelings back again. Adrian... I'm sorry. I am so sorry."

Adrian was surprised to find herself feeling a hint of pity as tears rolled down Jane's face. She had one fixated perception of hers that was being challenged with each passing moment. The girl that she felt wronged her was displaying a considerable amount of regret, but the odd thing was that she seemed to be missing a part of the story.

"Is abandonment the only thing you remember?" Adrian asked.

Jane looked at her, confused.

"Wow, you can't be serious. Jane, leaving me as my friend was one thing, why the fuck did you feel the need to humiliate me for it later on?"

"I don't understand."

"You've gotta be kidding me!" Adrian rolled her eyes and slammed her fist on the table.

"Adrian, I'm being honest here. What humiliation? I never told anyone about what happened between us."

Adrian's eyes widened. That couldn't possibly be true. Wasn't she siding with the other kids at her expense? Adrian was certain that Jane mentioned something to them, which is why they reacted that way.

"You told the other kids about me liking you!" Adrian accused.

Jane was taken aback by that.

"Adrian," she said, "I think there is a different version of the past you're trying to tell yourself. Yes, I did leave you as a friend. Yes, I did join the other mean kids and kept you away. But at no point did I ever mention about our moment together. I didn't even properly know about your…"

"Body? My unnatural body?"

"That's not what I meant."

"You don't seem to be meaning a lot of things, Jane. I'm really starting to question your honesty here."

"Just as much as I am wondering about your willingness to listen."

Both fell silent. Jane was displaying some backbone here. From the looks of it, if Jane wasn't being fully honest about her confession, she could've continued playing a sob story. The fact there was some rigidity on her end meant there was something that perhaps Adrian was indeed missing.

"Alright then," Adrian said. "Why did you and the other kids screw me over on the bonfire."

Jane's expression revealed that she knew where this was going. Her eyes had a sense of pity and compassion.

"Adrian, I didn't know that they were going to that."

"What?"

"I'm surprised that you assumed that I did."

It was going over Adrian's head, who stood up and started to pace left and right.

"You can't possibly be saying that!" Adrian accused. "I remember you being there!"

"You remember correctly, and I was there. I saw the whole thing play out. I wasn't part of it. It wasn't until the sick prank was over that I gave the group a hard time. You had left long before that. I even came over to your place after, and you were nowhere to be found. Your family even seemed quite distraught. It took a while before I realized that you didn't just run away, you left everything."

"A decision I couldn't be more proud of." Adrian seethed.

Jane looked at her former friend with a look of sympathy.

"Is that really true?" she asked.

"Excuse me! Why wouldn't I be? I've made a life for myself here. Call it whatever you want. I came here with nothing and now have a roof over my head. I made friends that are true to me. I fell in love and married a man who meant the world to me. What I could never dream of back in Thailand became a reality for me here!"

"If that were true, why do you still hold that spite? I just told you that I had no involvement in the sick stunt those kids did. Yet… you still…"

"You hurt me, Jane! Yes, you can apologize with your words! But you'll never feel the excruciating pain that I had to endure. Never once was there a day where I wasn't made to feel like a freak. You come along and make me feel important. You are kind and understanding how the hell was I not going to end up liking you? You were the first person that treated me like a decent human being! Fine, I was young and naïve and misconstrued my feelings. But for fuck's sake, couldn't you give me a chance to explain? That's all I ever wanted! A moment. A chance to make things right.

Even if you say that you weren't involved in making that ugly poster, you still left me. I needed my friend Jane. How the hell could you just go on living with that!"

Jane stood up and slowly began to pull up her sleeve. What Adrian saw shook her to the core. Jane's entire left wrist was infested with scars. There were so many that the sight of it would cause anyone to panic. Adrian felt herself almost stumble backwards before quickly regaining her balance.

Most of the scars had become one with the skin, but there were some hints of recent cuts. Adrian's eyes kept going from Jane's wrist to her face. The further Jane pulled her sleeve, the more scars began to show. They were present till her elbow.

Whatever anger Adrian had inside her completely subsided, as she found herself crying.

"I couldn't forgive myself for what I did for such a long time," Jane explained. "The guilt was so much, and I felt I deserved to be punished. I couldn't find you to make amends, so I just… felt that this was a way to keep myself in line. To just keep hurting myself because I betrayed my one friend.

Adrian, not a day has gone by when I haven't thought about you. Whenever a memory came running to me, all I could do was endure this heaviness in my chest. I'd cut myself, thinking it was the right way to go about it. I-"

Jane was stopped as Adrian revealed her scars on arm. Although not the same in terms of intensity and number, both were finally on the same page regarding something.

"I think I can relate to that as well." Adrian whimpered. "I know what that is like. I… I forgive you, Jane."

Jane jumped forward and hugged Adrian tightly. Both cried in one another's arms as the sky darkened, letting the forecasted rain finally fall upon the big apple.

Clara stared at Jimmy, annoyed by the fact that he had already sneaked at a slice. The buffoon sat opposite her at the diner, looking embarrassed.

"You just can't help yourself, can you?" she rolled her eyes.

"It's been almost an hour," Jimmy replied sadly. "And it's not easy fighting my tummy."

"It's never easy fighting with you on anything, big guy. Since self-restraint is not your best trait, I'm gonna try bringing yoga into your life."

"That stuff is for sissies."

Clara lay her head on the table, annoyed. Rising up, she noticed that Adrian was taking much longer than anticipated. The rain seemed to be picking up, too, and the last thing the girl wanted was the entire surprise going down the drain. She stared out of the window to see no sign of her.

"Did you get any text from Adrian-Hey? Hands off the food!"

"My bad. Tummy is growling."

"I'll be growling soon if you don't keep it together. This is the last time I'm ever leaving a sweet dish in front of you."

"It wasn't even sweet. It tastes like cheese."

"Yeah, I believe that's why they call it cheese cake!"

"Can I order something in the meantime while we wait then?"

"I ain't yo mama."

"You sure act like it."

"Say again?"

"Nothing. Nothing." Jimmy grumbled, making his way to the counter.

Clara went back to staring out of the window. New York was getting its usual bath from the sky, but it was definitely not going to be enough. Like most young girls wanting to get away from their small towns to the big city, Clara was exposed to a much uglier side of it. Luckily, with Adrian's help, she was already studying for her GED paper. If there was one thing she knew that would set her apart from the usual runaways, it was the fact she had some academic qualification to show for it.

Adrian mentioned college was a potential option, to which both shared a laugh. The tuition would take a lifetime to pay back. Yet, it didn't deter her from considering some option or another. She needed work and although the big city had plenty to offer, Clara wanted out of the underbelly of the city. Having been reliant on men giving her false hope, she knew she only herself to rely on. It was a relief when Adrian and Jimmy came around. Most people would toss her to the street at the slightest chance. These two were keepers.

Clara didn't just want to better things for herself but help Adrian and Jimmy move upwards. It would be nice to have a much better apartment where they wouldn't have to deal with the usual problems of drainage and flickering lights. For now, it seemed like a distant dream, but lately, she was feeling a bit optimistic.

Her eyes caught a familiar figure heading to the door, drenched from head to toe. With her was another face she had seen before but couldn't place. Clara stood up, relieved to see Adrian but freezing immediately. The blonde had returned. Clara dreaded that another angry reaction was coming her way. She stayed still as Adrian and the blonde came to her. The former hugged her tight, and from the look on her face, Clara assumed that Adrian was already in on the idea.

"What a wonderful cake you've... wait... did you start already?" Adrian asked.

"No, that's just... erm..."

"Hey, Adrian. You're here." Jimmy cheered louder than he should have. "I'm so sorry about... wait..."

Adrian took notice of how both Clara and Jimmy were staring in shock as Jane pulled down her hoodie.

"Hey," she greeted awkwardly. "Adrian told me about you two."

"Same here." The two said in unison.

Adrian, seeing this was not going to be a normal conversation, felt it was best to get to the point before everyone ended up eating in total silence.

"Yes," she said. "This is Jane, and we both just had a heart to heart an hour ago. Now, a lot has been let out, but there is still plenty more to do before things are clarified. For now, it's a rainy day, and I could use some cake."

Everyone took their place and sang Adrian her song. Some of the strangers at the neighboring tables applauded for her. Adrian experienced an epiphany as she took a bite of the cake. The universe had played one of its games. Right on the day she turned 32, someone from her past returned. Not only that, but she had some revelations about her past that she hadn't expected. It certainly shook her to the core, but after so long, she came to know that she wasn't the only one who suffered that day.

Jane's honesty opened an old wound in Adrian, but she resisted the temptation to stroke her own ego. Too much time had passed, and so much had happened. It felt unfair now to be petty. It certainly wasn't easy because there was some anger still lying within, but for now, at least she could let it out in a healthy manner.

"This cake is delicious." Jane complimented.

"It's plain cheesecake," Clara mentioned, not seeing the big deal.

"It's still pretty tasty. I can't remember the last time I had cake."

"You don't have birthdays?" Jimmy asked.

"Never celebrated, honestly. They never felt earned."

That certainly made everyone go quiet. Adrian decided to step in.

"Everyone follows the trend of letting New Year's Eve be the day to set resolutions." She spoke. "But I will make one now, as I enter a new year in my life. My first is to learn and become able to forgive."

Jane looked at her with a tearful smile, and both the women hugged, which certainly helped break the tension. Both Jimmy and Clara looked at one another and decided to go with it.

"My New Year resolution is to make sure Jimmy is never left alone with food." Clara toasted.

Everyone had a laugh at that. As the rain lessened outside, within the diner, four individuals shared jokes and stories and made the day worth remembering.

Chapter Ten

Adrian stood in front of her former group of LGBT members, knowing that a reaction was inevitable. After some time with therapy and getting feedback from the group, the divide couldn't be any more obvious. The polarization within the community bothered her, but she didn't want it hanging over her head for the rest of the time.

Having considered surgery and hormonal therapy, Adrian faced so many conflicting thoughts, and it upset her that people seemed entitled toto have a say regarding her life. Some labeled her as selfish and sent her kind back a hundred years. The others bombarded her with so much appreciation and support that it felt somewhat unreal and forced.

Having self-reflected in therapy and with some advice from Patricia and her friends, Adrian felt it was best to distance herself from the group until she was certain that it was her say in the end. Getting the surgery done was by far one of the toughest questions she had to ask. Having lived a life where everyone would stare at her, she felt that altering her appearance would change things for the better.

It wasn't until she met a former trans-gender man and woman who told her that despite them getting changes done to their body, it felt even more bothersome to look in the mirror and not recognize who was there. In the beginning, one could relish, but at one point, you return to questioning who is looking back at you. The mind is so ingrained with what we look like that, at times, it can get difficult to fathom what has happened.

It was Logan, former man turned woman, who put it best.

"Since childhood, you've seen one image of you in the mirror. One day, that changes. Because the brain is wired to recognize yourself in one way, it, at times, isn't ready to accept the changes. Yes, there will be days when you like what you see, but that itself is temporary. There will come a point where you will miss seeing the familiar. I changed myself to what I am now, but there are plenty of times when I see my reflection and cannot recognize who is looking back at me."

Logan's words really hit home. As much as she resented certain parts about herself, there was something scary about the possibility of experiencing that kind of identity crisis. Adrian had to struggle for many years when it came to who and what she was, but now she wanted to settle on a solution that would make the coming days easier.

During her time with Matthew, Adrian noticed that she started off feeling insecure, but her husband went on to make her feel beautiful. Whenever she was in his arms, nothing else mattered. It was this that made her realize how much the relationships around her shaped the perception she had about herself. Humans were social animals, and as much as she enjoyed her individualistic perspective, there would be times when she would appreciate the approval of others. The requirement was not to overdo that part.

Jane proved to be a surprising source of help. Having made amends, Adrian assumed that Jane would leave, but instead, she helped Adrian, Clara, and Jimmy find a better place for themselves. They moved out of the dilapidated dump to a cleaner and nicer environment.

"What did you say you do for a living?" Jimmy asked.

"Real estate." Jane winked. Everyone laughed at that.

The physical shift seemed to change the entire group as a collective. Clara garnered some courage and began to apply for a teaching job. She was put in charge of preschool school children. Although the pay was mediocre, she enjoyed working with children. Jimmy decided to leave behind his bouncer background and joined a gym as an instructor. Much to the surprise of everyone, he proved to be quite good at communicating instructions when it came to exercise.

Jane continued with her work in real estate, while Adrian found herself journalling a lot. Using anonymity as a tool, she began to pursue journalism while at the same time starting a food delivery service. Having worked in so many food-oriented places, it felt right to utilize those skills. She liked having her privacy while providing food to people. The new apartment had enough room for her to install a distinct kitchen of her own, and she thrived in making Thai-based food.

One day, after a long day of work, Jane visited, and Adrian entertained her with some herbal tea while the two talked about things. Adrian brought up her thoughts about getting the surgery done. It seemed closer to a possibility as some members of the group were willing to pitch in for it. Moved by their generosity, she still had some lingering doubt about their intent of charity. Was it because they genuinely cared for her well-being, or were they simply keen on getting some self-righteous kick out of it? Patricia was someone whom Adrian trusted the most, and even she felt it wasn't right of her to make a judgment on the matter. That made Adrian respect her more.

"Be honest with me, Jane," Adrian insisted. "Will the surgeries help?"

Jane took a sip of the tea, pondered for a moment and then began.

"I know why you want to do it," she explained. "If anything, a part of me would even encourage you to do it. But there is something that is being overlooked, and that is the relationship you have with yourself. For a long time, you were surrounded by people who didn't fully understand you, and that led them to be either afraid or cruel. But with time, you did start to find others who did get you. They accepted you and loved you for who you are. That brought up a new perspective in your life.

Matthew was a good example of this. You told me that he never made you feel out of place. He treated you like a person, not a tool. You even made friends along the way. Strangers gave you a helping hand in times of need. So much time has been spent in this body of yours that… changing it may change everything for both good and bad. It's a big step, Adrian, and it's not something anyone can adapt to in a matter of weeks, months, or even years. You will find yourself wondering who you are.

Everyone in life has that moment where they question if the grass is greener somewhere else. I found myself plenty of times. It's a tricky place to be because what feels crappy one day doesn't seem so bad the other. Now, this is not just a minor matter. This is your body. It's literally pieces of you that make you whole. One small cut affects the whole system. This is a surgery. It's gonna be deep cuts, stitches, torn skin, and God knows what. I don't want you feeling that after going through all of that, you find yourself missing what you once had."

"You seem pretty convinced that I would miss myself like this. Why?"

"There is a lot of difference between the Adrian I once knew and the one I'm sitting next to you. She used to walk with a hunch, you strut. She spoke so quietly while you articulated with ease. She was scared, you are brave. She assumed she didn't deserve good things; you fight to make things better. I feel… that the former insecure Adrian… is still whispering at the back of your mind. I worry how much she is influencing your decision."

Jane finished her tea and sat in a yoga pose. Whenever she said something with a lot of gravity, she had to breathe after. Adrian smiled at her. Even she was recollecting how Jane had changed. The one from years ago was quite the catch, eager and out there. This one was center and much more calm and cool.

"I never imagined a day where I'd say this, but… I am grateful you came back into my life." Adrian admitted.

The two gave each other a tight hug.

"I think I know why that former me still hangs around." Adrian realized.

"Why?"

"Because it still wants me to reach out to my family."

Jane looks at her, quite surprised.

"Of all the reasons," Jane admitted.

"I know. It bothers me a lot sometimes. I ran away, leaving many things behind. My assumption was that coming here would help me forget, and it certainly did to an extent. Landing here opened my mind to a new world, but a part of me still lingers there. If I am to truly decide on a future, I can't do it without confronting my past."

Adrian had never seen Jane look so proud of her.

"Do you want me to come with you back to Thailand?" she asked.

"No. I appreciate it, but you have work here. This is something I have to confront on my own. The surgeries can wait. I want to meet my family and come to terms with what happened. Regardless of whether it will go good or bad."

"You truly are one helluva woman, Adrian."

Adrian was packing her things as Jimmy carried the big bags to the Uber outside. Clara wouldn't stop crying while she helped getting all the things together.

"Oh, I'm not going forever, Clara." Adrian sighed.

"I know." the girl sobbed. "It's just so far away, and I don't even know when you'll come back."

"A few weeks, dear. It'll be over before you even know it."

Adrian gave her a tight hug and made her way out while everyone followed. Patricia gave her some cookies for the trip.

"I hope you find what you're looking for," she assured her.

Jane put her hand around Clara to comfort her, which helped. Adrian hugged them both. Jimmy looked a little grumpy but didn't say much. Adrian kissed his cheek, which made him blush. After saying plenty of goodbyes, Adrian got into the car and waved as the car drove off.

"You all take care of one another, okay?" she shouted, rolling down the window.

"We will," they said in unison.

Sitting back, Adrian watched parts of the city pass her by. It was a strange feeling that it would be some time before she would see this again. She had plenty of the country, but this time, there was an ocean to cross. Something about the uncertainty of what was to come bothered her, but it also gave her more eagerness. A step was being taken that was unlike any other, and she knew that having learned to forgive was what brought her to this decision.

Her parting words with Matthew sunk in and deep, and it was no coincidence that Jane would return to her life. Now, those things had led Adrian to confront the past, and that could set things in motion for what she wanted to do in the future. Forgiveness and acceptance, truly was the most healing experience of her life.

"Expecting some traffic on the route, Miss." the driver said. "Airport tends to be busy at this hour. You heading for vacation?"

"No," Adrian smiled, feeling an elation in her chest. "I'm going home."

Thank You!

Milton Keynes UK
Ingram Content Group UK Ltd.
UKHW020940190324
439594UK00002B/18